This book is due for return on or before the last date shown below.

AN ANGLO-NORMAN MONASTERY

BRIDGETOWN PRIORY AND THE ARCHITECTURE OF THE AUGUSTINIAN CANONS REGULAR IN IRELAND

Tadhg O'Keeffe

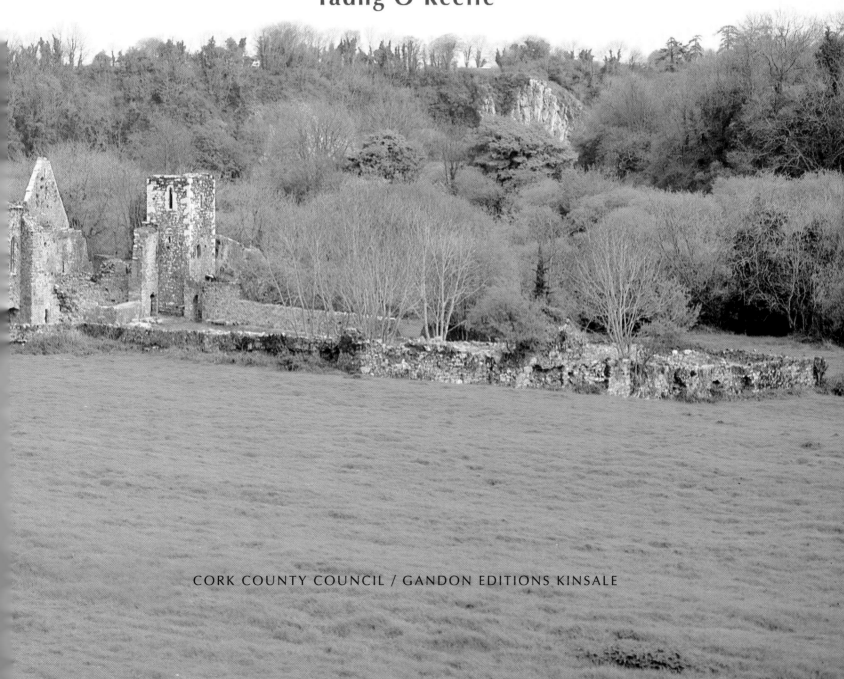

CORK COUNTY COUNCIL / GANDON EDITIONS KINSALE

AN ANGLO-NORMAN MONASTERY
Bridgetown Priory and the Architecture of the Augustinian Canons Regular in Ireland
by Tadhg O'Keeffe

Published by Cork County Council and Gandon Editions
© The author, 1999. All rights reserved.

ISBN 0946641 803

design	John O'Regan (© Gandon, 1999)
production	Nicola Dearey, Gandon Editions
printing	Betaprint, Dublin
distribution	Gandon Editions and its overseas agents

illustrations	Michael Herity, David Jennings, *archaeological photography*
	John Searle, *architectural photography*
	Niamh Ó Broin, *archaeological drawings*
	Antoinette O'Neill, *architectural drawings*
	see page 9 for other illustration credits

cover	View southwards along vaulted cloister passage
cartouche	Stone head carved in oolithic limestone
frontispiece	Bridgetown Priory from the south-west

CORK COUNTY COUNCIL, County Hall, Cork
tel +353 (0)21-276891 / *fax* +353 (0)21-276321 / *e-mail* cosec@corkcoco.ie
web-site www.corkcoco.com

GANDON EDITIONS, Oysterhaven, Kinsale, Co Cork
tel +353 (0)21-770830 / *fax* +353 (0)21-770755 / *e-mail* gandon@tinet.ie
web-site www.gandon-editions.com

Contents

FOREWORD   7

ACKNOWLEDGEMENTS   8

INTRODUCTION   11

1   THE RULE OF ST AUGUSTINE
    AND THE MEDIEVAL IRISH CHURCH   15
    The monastic spirit and the world of the Middle Ages

2   THE BLACK CANONS AT BRIDGETOWN   25

3   THE MONASTIC RULE AND THE MASON'S RULER   49
    The layout and building history of Bridgetown Priory

4   AUGUSTINIAN ARCHITECTURAL IDENTITIES   107
    Bridgetown Priory in context

5   MISSION ABANDONED   147
    The afterlife of Bridgetown Priory

SELECTED BIBLIOGRAPHY   149

LIST OF ILLUSTRATIONS   152

NOTES AND REFERENCES   154

Foreword

THE PRESERVATION AND CARE OF ANCIENT MONUMENTS HAS BEEN A DUTY OF Cork County Council since its foundation in 1899. Developing from the local authority's original role as custodian of graveyards and the monuments contained within them, this duty has evolved, expanded and been redefined over time by both National Monuments and planning legislation.

Cork County Council has had a long association with the Augustinian priory at Bridgetown which is one of a number of archaeological and architectural monuments in its care. Representing an Irish expression of a European architectural idiom, Bridgetown Priory is one of the finest Anglo-Norman monasteries in Ireland. This, combined with the monument's beautiful setting on the river Blackwater, provides the modern visitor with a magical connection with the past.

As one of the most significant and extensive monuments in our care, the site has been the focus of conservation works since 1992. The first step in this process was a careful historical and physical investigation of the site, commissioned from Dr Tadhg O'Keeffe. This book represents the culmination of his work.

Cork County Council are proud to be associated with this book, and hope that it will heighten the awareness and appreciation of our unique archaeological and architectural heritage.

KEVIN MURPHY
Chairman, Cork County Council

MAURICE MOLONEY
County Manager

February 1999

Acknowledgements

ORK COUNTY COUNCIL'S INITIATIVE IN UNDERTAKING THE SURVEY AND EXCA-vation of historic sites in the county, and in making the results of that work available in published form, is deserving of very high praise from all who take pleasure in Ireland's heritage. This publication owes much to the vision and commitment of the former County Manager, Noel Dillon, and the members of the Historic Monuments Advisory Committee for Cork. I have particular pleasure, both personal and professional, in acknowledging the contribution to this project of John Ludlow of the Architects Department, Cork County Council. This publication owes much to his tireless and patient devotion to Bridgetown.

Special thanks are due also to Michael Monk, Dept of Archaeology, University College Cork, who was an effective and sympathetic liaison with the County Council; to David Kelly, who provided advice on structural matters arising out of both the survey and the excavation; and to Dr Colin Rynne, who first pushed this text on the road to publication. John Irwin, Dept of Engineering, University College Cork, organised and supervised an EDM survey of the ruins, the results of which form the basis of the site plan published here. A detailed survey of the priory was carried out with professional assistance from Eamonn Cotter and Debbie O'Sullivan, and the excavation in 1992 was conducted with assistance from Jacinta Kiely (supervisor), Catherine Burke, Jimmy Corbett, Dermot Doggett, Carmel Joyce and Eileen Magner. Chuck Leese and Roger Janman, stonemasons on the site, have contributed enormously through their observations to my reading of the building. Their work continues to reveal the structural complexity of the priory. The survey of the earthworks beside the priory was conducted by Paul Synnott. Kieran Hore offered valuable help with the history of the priory.

I am grateful to the staff of the libraries of Trinity College Dublin, the Royal Irish Academy, Dublin, and the Courtauld Institute of Art, University of London. I have special pleasure in acknowledging the assistance given to me by Siobhán de hÓir and Orna Sommerville in the library of the Royal Society of Antiquaries of Ireland, Richard Clutterbuck who undertook cartographical research on my behalf in the National Library of Ireland, Christy Roche for his observations on the priory, Gerard Crotty for advise on the heraldic device on the canopied tomb in the choir, and Dr Stephen Mandell for his identification of the oolithic limestone at the priory.

Photographs, site plans and architectural fragments from Dermot Twohig's work on the site in the late 1970s were made available to me by Dr Elizabeth Shee Twohig, Department of Archaeology, University College Cork, to whom I am most grateful. My thanks also to Professor Michael Herity, Department of Archaeology, University College Dublin, for his aerial photography of Bridgetown (illustration numbers 13, 25), to John Searle for his photographs at the site (cover, 2, 5, 17, 22-24, 30-34, 39, 40, 45, 48-51, 59-64, 68, 137, 145-147), to David Jennings, Department of Archaeology, UCD, for his photography at Bridgetown and at other sites (16, 41-43, 47, 52, 53, 56-58, 65, 72, 114), to Dúchas, the Heritage Service (8, 9, 21, 36, 44, 46, 75, 80, 81, 95, 96, 101, 108-13, 115, 120, 121, 123, 127, 134, 139, 140, 142-44), and to the Courtauld Institute of Art for permission to reproduce their photographs (37, 38, 77, 82, 118). The site plans are the work of Antoinette O'Neill; the remainder of the drawings are by Niamh Ó Broin.

Finally, special debts are owed to Mrs Mary Dulohery – whose lands adjoin the ruins – for being a generous and interested host throughout, and to my wife, Margaret, for her support during the writing of this monograph, and for casting her critical eye over its pages.

———

Dedication
IN MEMORY OF TIM

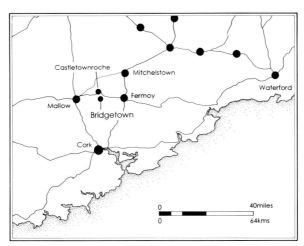

3 Location map of
   Bridgetown Priory

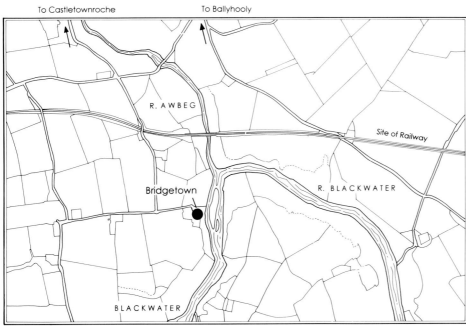

Introduction

BRIDGETOWN PRIORY HAS STOOD WITNESS TO COMINGS AND GOINGS ALONG THE rivers Blackwater and Awbeg for nearly eight centuries [**3**]. Dissolved as a monastery five and a half centuries ago, the ruins were for many years enveloped in a cape of luxuriant ivy which blended into the greenery of the setting. Cleared of that mantle and with its walls now conserved, Bridgetown takes its place among the finest examples of Anglo-Norman monastic houses in Ireland [**2**].

Bridgetown Priory was built by canons regular of St Augustine – priests (canons) who lived in community according to the Rule (hence 'regular') of St Augustine. Popularly known as the 'black canons' on account of their habit, they were one of the many religious groupings which emerged in the 11th century as a major vehicle for the reform of religious life in Europe in the aftermath of many centuries of decay. The Rule of St Augustine provided a model by which adherents to the ideal of monastic life could successfully negotiate the Present in their quest for the After. The rush to join monastic orders such as the Cistercians, Cluniacs and Augustinians, or, to our 20th-century eyes, slightly more obscure orders such as the Gilbertines, Trinitarians and Premonstratensians, is among the most remarkable phenomena of the Middle Ages. The timetable of work and prayer which the communities followed may have seemed as demanding to novices then as it does to us now, but once accustomed to it, life within the cloister was an existence without challenge, without danger. This must have been part of its attraction, as literally hundreds of thousands of people across Europe joined monasteries in the high Middle Ages, many of them as young adults on the cusp of maturity.

Whether one was a canon regular, a friar or a nun, daily life within a monastery was highly regulated. All the monastic orders conformed to a basic pattern of life and worship within their cloisters, but the nature of the monastic involvement with the world beyond varied from one order to another; some placed the provision of pastoral care high on their agenda, whereas others operated in comparative isolation from secular communities. What all the monastic orders did have in common, however, was their capacity to draw considerable human resources from the secular world, and to compensate that world with art and learning, and, for those wealthy enough to be benefactors of monasteries, a route by which salvation could be achieved.

Between the 12th and the 16th centuries, Ireland was host to no less than eighteen different monastic groupings, all them reaching Ireland from Europe, where they originated in a Christian environment heavily indebted to Ireland and Irish missionaries of an earlier age for its health and its personality. It was the reform of the Irish Church in the early 12th century which opened the door to this European monasticism, and by the middle of that century, even before the Anglo-Normans arrived, there were communities of Augustinians, Benedictines and Cistercians in the country. Of the principal orders, the Franciscans and Dominicans followed in the next century, enticed here by Anglo-Norman patronage.

The Augustinians founded more monastic houses in Ireland than any of the other orders: at least 144 monastic establishments of varying type and status – abbeys, priories, friaries, cells – can be attributed to the order, among them some of Ireland's very finest medieval remains, such as the priories of Kells, Co Kilkenny, and Athassel, Co Tipperary. Despite this, the Augustinians trail rather timidly behind the Franciscans and Cistercians in the historiography of medieval monasticism, and specifically of monastic architecture, in Ireland.[1] The problem lies partly with the slow creep of scholarship, but the nature of the Rule of St Augustine itself is not without blame. First, part of the attraction of life as an Augustinian was the flexibility of the Rule which bears his name. Augustine did not actually write a Rule: what passed as his Rule was simply the adoption – indeed, the paraphrasing – of his stated views on communal life. Secondly, for those orders, such as the Cistercians, who chose to live in comparative isolation from the secular world, the layout of monastic buildings was as highly regulated as the monastic day itself, but Augustinians generally regarded pastoral care in the community as an important pursuit and so were less bound to life within the cloister, thus allowing their monastic buildings to be laid out with less consistency. There is, then, no such thing as a typical Augustinian monastery, within Ireland or without, and so a study of Augustinian monastic architecture in Ireland would thus be nothing less than a study of the entire spectrum of architectural forms and sculptural motifs used in the ecclesiastical environment of medieval Ireland.

One approach to the daunting task of uncovering the identity, or identities, of Augustinian architecture in medieval Ireland is through monographs on their individual buildings, monographs in which the description and analysis of architecture is accompanied by both historical and archaeological assessments.[2] This particular study of a foundation of Augustinian canons regular in north Cork – Bridgetown Priory – should be viewed as one step in the unravelling of the architectural personality of the Rule of St Augustine in Ireland. Its principal aim is the further documentation and interpretation of a monastery which has been a subject of research at both ends of this century [4] but which is still relatively little known.[3] It has the additional aim of allowing this monastery be a point of departure from which the corpus of architecture in Ireland for which the Augustinian canons were responsible, particularly those operating under Anglo-Norman patronage, may be made intelligible. This book's target audience is simply those who enjoy the experience of exploring buildings, whether they are scholars professionally engaged in the study of the Middle Ages, or visitors from walks of life on which the Middle Ages rarely impinge. If this book helps make Ireland's monastic buildings accessible and enjoyable, while offering at the same time a sense of the historical and religious environment in which these wonderful monasteries were built, it will have fulfilled my modest ambition for it.

———

4　A plan of Bridgetown Priory drawn by Revd M Horgan early this century[4]

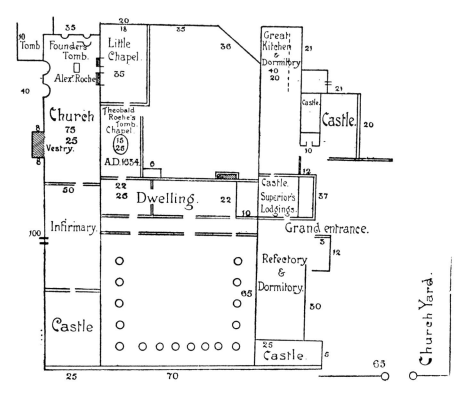

 # 1

The Rule of St Augustine and the Medieval Irish Church

The monastic spirit and the world of the Middle Ages

MONASTICISM IS ALMOST AS OLD AS CHRISTIANITY ITSELF. ALTHOUGH A metropolitan religion in origin, and one with a strong evangelical dimension from the outset, Christianity encouraged in its adherents the ultimate of denials: for those who chose the path of monasticism, literally the path of 'one who dwells alone', isolation and deprivation promised the accelerated arrival of salvation. The eremitical lifestyle was the purest ideal of monasticism. Christ himself had spent forty days and nights of penance alone in the desert, withstanding temptation after temptation. His successors were to emulate his achievement with such staggering bouts of self-denial as Simeon who sat at the top of a pillar for forty-seven years. Less harsh was coenobitic monasticism – communal monasticism, essentially – which allowed monks the security of each other's company and the potential to achieve *en masse* what each was less capable of achieving alone. The Acts of the Apostles provided some legitimacy: 'All who believed were together and had all things in common. And sold their possessions and goods and parted them to all men as every man had need.'[5] Despite the initial popularity of emeriticism and a revival of its fortunes in the 11th century, it was the coenobitic tradition of monastic life which proved to have longer-term appeal, as Christianity, no longer a troublesome and unintelligible cult but the official Roman religion from the early 4th century, moved out of the dry, humid climes of the remote Roman province of Palestine, colonised the Empire, and eventually seeped into lands beyond the Empire's fringe, such as Ireland.[6] The father of coenobitism is widely regarded as Pachomius (*c*.292-346), an Egyptian conscript in the Roman army who, upon converting, founded a coenobitic monastery in the upper Nile valley and saw that it ran according to a Rule. The coenobitic movement established by St Basil the Great of Caeseria (*c*.330-79) in Asia Minor, which drew inspiration from the Pachomian model, was much nearer to the monastic convention of later medieval times, with power and responsibility vested in a monastic superior. The comparable Rule devised by St Benedict of Nursia (*c*.480-550) had a more

profound impact on later western Christendom. Two and a half centuries after Benedict's death, Charlemagne favoured St Benedict's Rule for monasteries within his Frankish realms, and even dispatched an abbot to Benedict's old monastery of Monte Cassino to obtain details of its comprehensive strictures on the obligations and organisation of daily life, on the layout of the monastery, and on recruitment and training of new members. When the year 1000 arrived and Apocalypse had not accompanied it, as had been feared, the world was covered, in the memorable words of Ralph Glabar,[7] with 'a white cloak of churches'; many of those churches were monastic and invariably their communities drew guidance from St Benedict's Rule.

The euphoria which must have greeted the deliverance of the world from the fulfilment of the terrifying prophesies in the Book of Revelations was but one element of the ecclesiastical rejuvenation which led to the widespread building of churches in the 1000s. An overhaul of the institution of the Church was badly needed in the 11th century: the papacy had long been in decay, secular interests had intruded into Church affairs, and abuses such as simony and nepotism were widespread among the clergy. The Gregorian Reform of the middle of the 11th century addressed these issues, promulgating the view that indiscipline among the clergy could best be countered by encouraging the adoption of monastic regulations. What was advocated, in other words, was that clerics should live as *canonici regulares*, priests (canons) following a monastic Rule. This was an idea with a long history. Augustine, bishop of Hippo in north Africa between *c*.395 and 430, had advocated the idea of priests living in community and relinquishing their personal property, and when he became coadjutor bishop of Hippo he turned his episcopal residence into a house for a monastic community. When the Lateran Council of 1059 authorised the adoption of a common life by the clergy, it was St Augustine's thinking on the matter which shaped their thoughts and actions.

Unlike St Benedict, St Augustine did not actually write a Rule. What became known as the *Regula Sancti Augustini* was a conflation of several texts. One was *Letter 211*, a letter he wrote in 423 advising a nunnery in which his sister was superior on appropriate monastic conduct; indeed, *Letter 211* is the only commentary on the practice of religious life which can be attributed to Augustine's own hand. The second text was the *Ordo monasterii*, which was prepared by Augustine's friend Alypius and which may have been shaped to its final form by Augustine himself. Finally, there was the *Praeceptum*, a series of guidelines on such matters as liturgy, clothing, food and manual labour, which Augustine himself had advocated for his own community in Hippo.[8]

Adherence to the Rule of St Augustine meant the best of both worlds. The Rule carried the authority of a man of great sanctity, an intellectual heavyweight and one of Christendom's most revered figures, but, as it was not the written word of Augustine himself, a certain latitude was permissible in the

6 Drawing of Hugh of St Victor
A leading theologian and biblical scholar of the 12th century, Hugh founded the famous school at the Parisian abbey. This image is adapted from a 13th-century manuscript of his, *De arca morali* (Bodleian Library, Oxford).

practice of it. Some of its adherents favoured the *vita apostolica*, which entailed the dispensing of pastoral care in parish churches, cathedrals and hospitals. The Rule's flexibility not only allowed for this, but it also facilitated its rapid spread from the start of the 12th century. Others drawn to monastic life found the idea of contemplative life within the cloister more favourable, and here the Rule was equally accommodating.

Such diversity in the adherence to the Rule is apparent from the start of the 12th century in two northern French monasteries, St Nicholas in Arrouaise and St Victor in Paris, both of which had their particular observances of the Rule closely followed by communities elsewhere, including Ireland. The monastery at Arrouaise, founded by three hermits about 1090, followed the Rule very strictly, placing utmost emphasis on contemplation and liturgy. Essential elements of the Arroasian (or Arrouaisian) observance, such as the concept of the General Chapter, the annual meeting at Arrouaise of the superiors of the monastery's daughter houses,[9] were borrowed from the Cistercians, an order founded in Burgundy in 1098 by Robert of Molesme and dependent on the Rule of St Benedict. By contrast with Arrouaise, St Victor in Paris, founded in 1108 by William de Champeaux after he had resigned as archdeacon of Paris and retired from his teaching duties in the cathedral school there, was a centre of intellectual pursuits [**6**], and it enjoyed generous royal funding. Cistercian influence can also be observed in this Parisian house: there was an annual General Chapter for about a century after its establishment, and William himself chose to be buried in his Victorine habit in a specially built mortuary chapel at the Cistercian house of Clairvaux.[10] The founder of the Victorine house of Wigmore (Herefordshire), Oliver de Merlemond, had stayed at St Victor in Paris in the 1140s, and it clearly made a positive impression on him:[11] he 'examined and carefully considered all things which he saw in the guesthouse, the cloister and the choir, and particularly the service which was performed around the altar, and his heart was moved by the orderliness which he saw in all places.' The order survived until the 19th century, and its Paris house, extensively rebuilt in the 16th century, was demolished.[12]

St Augustine's writings became the foundation on which other groupings of canons regular were built, although again with a strong Cistercian input. They include the Order of Prémontré – the Premonstratensian canons or 'white canons' – which was founded by Norbert of Xanten (*c*.1080-1134), and the Gilbertines, a mixed order of canons regular, nuns and lay brethren, named after St Gilbert. Adoption of the Rule was not confined to canons regular. Among the mendicant (literally 'begging') friars who followed the Rule were the Dominican friars, founded by Dominic de Guzman (*c*.1170-1221), and the Augustinian friars, originally hermits in northern Italy who, following the guidance of Pope Alexander IV in 1256, united under the authority of the Rule of St Augustine but modelled their life according to the Constitutions of the Dominican Order.

———

The 12th-century reform of the Irish Church

The Irish Church did not remain unaffected for long by these 11th and 12th-century developments in mainland Europe. Lapses in the rigour and sanctity of monastic practise, which prompted the papacy to instigate a reform of the Church in Continental Europe, were also of concern to the Irish clerics at the close of the 11th century, and by the middle of the following century the Irish Church had embraced the spirit of reform.[13] During the 10th and 11th centuries the close contacts between Ireland and Europe which had been established prior to the Vikings were renewed, and not only did Irishmen travel abroad to serve in Continental monasteries, but knowledge of events overseas spread back to Ireland and were sometimes considered significant enough for mention in the annalistic sources.

Irish royalty frequently undertook pilgrimages in the 11th century. In 1026, for example, the king of Cenel Conaill went on pilgrimage to Clonfert, then to Iona and then to Rome, while Sitric, king of Dublin, went to Rome with the king of Brega in 1028. Such royal pilgrimages would, from about 1050 onwards, have brought Irishmen into contact with the reforms of Leo IX and his successors, but while exposure to the reforming environment of mainland Europe stoked the conscience of the Irish Church – particularly through the travels of St Malachy – it was the Anglo-Norman Church in England which initially provided Ireland with its new direction, as is discussed below.

The reform of the Irish Church involved the installation of a new diocesan network [7]. This was first apparent in the Hiberno-Scandinavian towns where the bishops had been trained in Anglo-Norman houses such as Worcester and Canterbury. Synods at which the diocesan system with its fixed number of bishops was organised were held at Rathbreasail (probably in Co Cork) in 1111, and at Kells, Co Meath, in 1152.

The reform also introduced the monastic orders into Ireland, and here the main player was St Malachy of Armagh. Ordained a priest in 1119 at the age of twenty-five, by 1124 he was abbot of Bangor. By the following year he had ascended the ranks of the Irish Church to become bishop of Down, becoming archbishop of Armagh in 1132, and resigning that post to resume his work in Down diocese in 1137. On his return to Bangor, Malachy established a house of canons regular; this was not his first such act of patronage, as his biographer, St Bernard of Clairvaux, makes clear.[14] The new church, consecrated by Archbishop Cellach at Armagh in 1126 and dedicated to SS Peter and Paul, may have adopted the Rule of St Augustine at Malachy's behest after he had become Archbishop around 1132.

Malachy may also have been instrumental in the adoption of the Rule in the refounded abbey of Cong, Co Mayo, whence a community of canons regular brought the Rule southwards to Cork in 1134. Malachy had been in Munster in 1127, where he encountered Cormac Mac Carthaig, and with

7   Doorty Cross, Kilfenora, Co Clare
The carving of a bishop on the shaft of this early 12th-century High Cross reflects the creation after 1111 of the new diocesan network.

Cormac's assistance he established the now lost *monasterium Ibarense*,[15] probably as a house of Augustinian canons regular. While in Munster, Malachy may well have persuaded the native monastic communities at places like Lorrha, Co Tipperary, to follow the example of Bangor and to join the congregation of Augustinian houses.

Malachy's penchant for reformed monasticism was not restricted to the canons regular. Monks from the Benedictine abbey of Savignac, founded in 1127, established a house at Erenagh in the diocese of Down in 1127, clearly with the approval of Malachy. It was later destroyed by John de Courcy and replaced with the Cistercian abbey of Inch; indeed, the Savignac congregation had been merged with the Cistercians in 1147. The Benedictines were already in Ireland. In the late 11th century, a community of Benedictines, about whom virtually nothing is known, ran a hospital in Dublin, while Benedictines from Regensburg in Bavaria established bases in Rosscarbery, Co Cork, and Cashel.[16] The Benedictines were not to feature prominently in later Irish monastic history. Malachy also brought the Cistercians to Ireland, having encountered the order – and its leading light, St Bernard of Clairvaux – in 1139 while travelling to Rome.[17] One might describe the Cistercians as the first substantial new colonial presence on the island since the Vikings, whereas the Augustinian Rule was adopted by existing monastic communities.

In 1140 Malachy visited Arrouaise in north-east France. The observance of the Rule of St Augustine at Arrouaise was austere after the Cistercian model, and the houses of Arroasian congregation, like those of the Cistercians, held a General Chapter at the mother house.[18] Malachy was clearly impressed by what he saw; he had the Rule and the details of its observance copied and brought back to Ireland, where he persuaded a number of religious communities to adopt them.

The idea of having a conventual church serve as a cathedral, with its

8   St Mary's Priory, Louth
In 1242, apparently the centenary of its foundation, a Great Chapter of the Arroasians was held at the priory of Louth, with new reliquaries made for the occasion. The present church was probably built after 1312 when fire destroyed the original priory.

abbot as bishop and its monks serving as the chapter, was a peculiarly Anglo-Saxon phenomenon, and by 1066 there were four examples, three of which – Canterbury, Winchester and Worcester – were to provide bishops-elect for the Hiberno-Scandinavian towns.[19] The Normans adopted the idea, and by 1133 more than half the cathedrals of England were served by monastic orders, all Benedictines except Carlisle, which was Augustinian.[20] Although the principal church of the Arroasian observance in Ireland, at Louth, acted as the cathedral church for its diocese [8], Malachy was generally unsuccessful in persuading cathedral clergy in Ireland to follow the Augustinian Rule [9].[21]

The Arroasian observance was a northern phenomenon in Ireland: even Cork remained unattached after its mother house, Cong, had converted to the Arroasian observance. In England, where the adoption of regular life had followed a similar path (the house of St Botulph in Colchester, for example, was a secular college founded in 1095 which was converted by 1107 into a community of canons regular[22]), many of the Augustinian houses also followed the Arroasian observance. Upon their arrival in Ireland in the late 12th century, the Anglo-Normans perpetuated the Arroasian connection, although curiously the observance still only hesitantly spread southwards into Munster.[23]

The Rule of St Augustine was a godsend to those monastic communities of 12th-century Ireland which wished to embrace the spirit of reform but which were unwilling to capitulate entirely to the new episcopal authorities. By its very flexibility, St Augustine's Rule allowed native Irish monastic communities, long unaccustomed to the apostolic life, to engage fully in the new spirit of reform.

Canons Regular and Anglo-Norman patrons in Ireland

Considerable stimulus for reform of the Irish Church came from the two great prelates of the late 11th and early 12th-century Anglo-Norman Church – Lanfranc and Anselm.[24] Their own reforming credentials were impeccable: Lanfranc had, for example, founded a hospital in Canterbury as early as 1087 in which there were six canons regular, while Anselm had advised the eremitical community of Llanthony in the Black Mountains between England and Wales to become canons regular. That community was later to hold extensive Irish estates.[25]

The English Church had experienced revival shortly before 1000, and whether it was in need of renewed reform under the Normans in the late 1000s is open to question. The Normans themselves had embraced reform in their homeland of Normandy a short time prior to embarking for Hastings in 1066. The main players in Normandy were from the Italian world (Lanfranc was from Pavia; Anselm had roots in Aosta; William of Dijon, abbot of Fécamp

9   Annaghdown, Co Galway
     Senior clergy in Ireland were resistant to the idea of having monastic chapters serving their cathedrals, and thus monastic communities living close to the cathedrals had their own churches. At Annaghdown, a large priory of Augustinian canons regular (top) and a church of Premonstratensian canons (bottom right) are located close to a small cathedral church (far left).

10   An 18th-century image of a Victorine canon[29]

from 1001 to 1031 and the founding father of Norman reform, was a native of Volpiano in Piedmont, and his successor at Fécamp was from Ravenna), but the reform had the model of Cluny, the great Burgundian monastery, at its heart.[26] Following their success at Hastings, the Normans introduced reform into England from their homeland, replacing senior Anglo-Saxon clergy with their own clergy (though not immediately), and eventually replacing older Anglo-Saxon buildings.[27] They also enticed communities from older monastic houses in Normandy to England, with promises of endowments of English churches. This process of establishment of new Norman monasteries in England was not at the initiative of the monastic communities themselves, but was the product of deliberate and sometimes strategic patronage by the Norman aristocrats. Many of the new monasteries were Cluniac, and this affiliation is largely because the mother house at Cluny was well established as a great reforming centre. Cluniac houses in England commonly chose vacant sites, thus avoiding the need to reorganise older Anglo-Saxon establishments.

Anglo-Normans were active patrons of new Augustinian houses in Ireland, most of them priories rather than abbeys.[28] All these new foundations followed the Arroasian observance, apart from eight foundations which adopted the stricter variation on the Rule which was practised by the Augustinian congregation of St Victor in Paris [**10**, **11**].

21

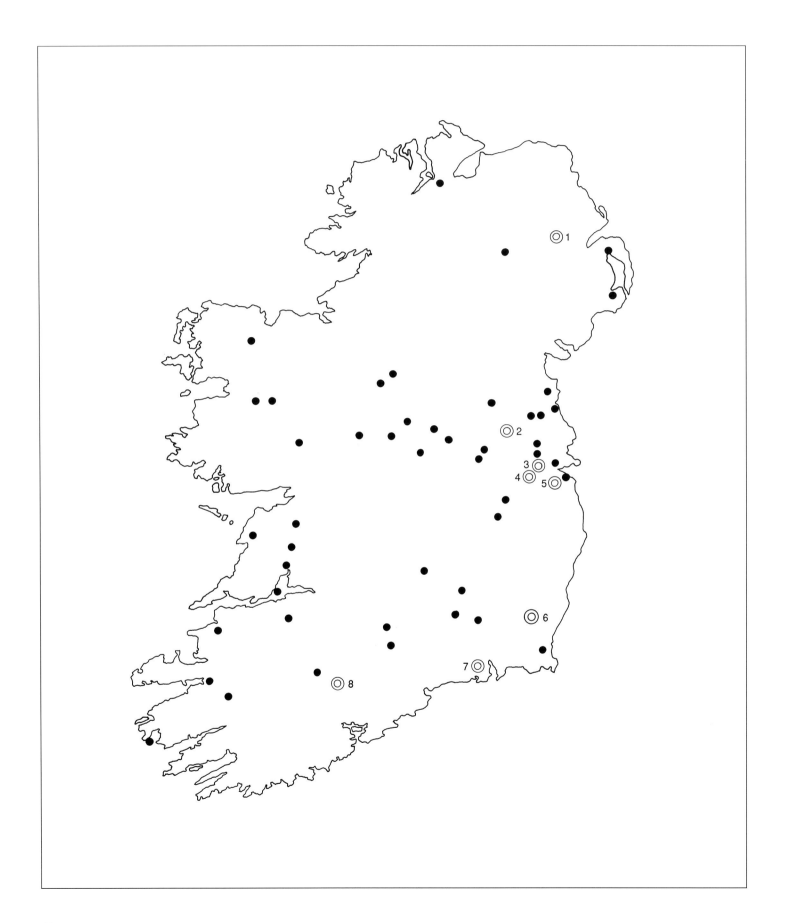

11   New Augustinian houses
in Ireland, 1169-1320

Open circles represent houses of the
Victorine congregation.[30]

1   Muckamore, Co Antrim
2   Newtown Trim, Co Meath
3   St Catherine's, Dublin
4   St Wolstan's, Co Kildare
5   St Thomas the Martyr, Dublin
6   Enniscorthy, Co Wexford
7   Waterford
8   Bridgetown, Co Cork

As in England, the map of monasticism in medieval Ireland was created less by monastic communities themselves than by patrons.[31] Many factors contributed to the popularity of the Augustinians among patrons. Prior to the Cistercians, there were few monastic movements to whom secular lords could provide patronage, even in England, where the Cluniacs had established an early hold thanks to their involvement in the reform of Normandy churches. Indeed, when the Cistercians did arrive in Ireland with their offer of an ascetic life, patrons remained attracted to the Augustinians. They could be relied upon to look after pastoral needs, and their new foundations required less resources than was necessary for Cluniacs, Benedictines or Cistercians.[32] Augustinians were, it seems, even preferred to the Cistercians in frontier areas to which the Cistercians were especially well suited.[33] In England the Augustinians enjoyed considerable royal patronage in the first few decades of the 12th century,[34] after which the numbers of new houses decreases, but in post-1169 Ireland it was the lesser magnates who were attracted to them,[35] among them the founder of Bridgetown Priory, Alexander fitz Hugh [**12**].

———

12   Alexander fitz Hugh?

This head, carved in oolithic limestone imported in the 13th century from south-western Britain, is conceivably from an early effigial tomb and it may represent Alexander fitz Hugh, the priory's founder. Effigies of secular lords are actually rare in Ireland before the close of the 13th century.

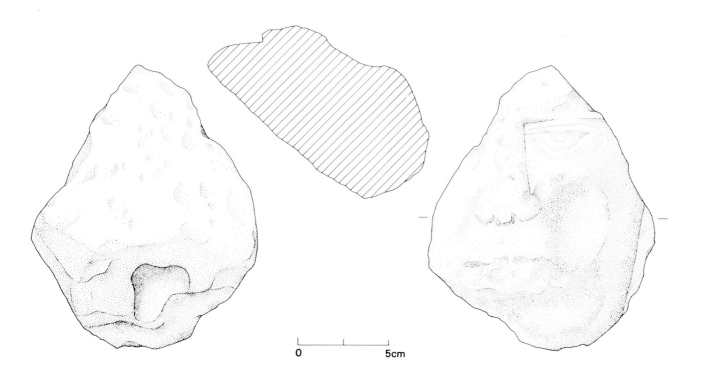

0   5cm

✠ 2

The Black Canons at Bridgetown

WHEN, IN MAY 1169, ROBERT FITZ STEPHEN DISEMBARKED THE BOAT which had carried him from Milford Haven onto the sandy beach of Bannow Bay, he, no more than those Irish annalists who recorded the landing of his mercenary troupe with casual disregard, could scarcely have realised that he was participating in the opening act of a drama which, two years later, would bring Henry II to Ireland, and, in turn, bring much of Ireland firmly within the embrace of the Angevin world.[36] If we are to believe his portrayal by his half-nephew, Giraldus Cambrensis, chronicler of the early history of the Anglo-Norman involvement in Ireland, Robert had all the qualities we may reasonably expect in a conquistador: strength, physical attractiveness, generosity. But he also had a fondness – and this was a failing in Giraldus's eyes – for women and wine.[37] Robert came to Ireland having been released from incarceration in Cardigan, the northerly extremity of the Norman colony which stretched along the Welsh littoral. Wales had never been completely incorporated within the Norman polity, and those Norman settlements which were established in that long finger of land between Monmouth and Cardigan were a breeding ground for men such as Robert, men who knew themselves to be at the periphery of the Norman world, men who saw that all the fertile land in the narrow corridors between the mountains and the sea was taken up, thus leaving little opportunity for them to carve out decent estates for themselves, and men for whom the potential spoils of a trip to Ireland would have outweighed whatever dangers might be involved. Robert acquitted himself very well in the three years he spent in Ireland following his arrival at Bannow, with the capture of Wexford featuring prominently in the list of his achievements. Indeed, among the first wave of Norman adventurers in Ireland, only Richard fitz Clare (Strongbow), the Earl of Pembroke, appears to have had a higher profile than Robert. In 1172 Robert departed Ireland to fulfil his feudal obligation of royal service in England and France. Milo de Cogan, who had come to Ireland in the train of Strongbow in 1170, and had risen to be the governor of Dublin, was also recalled from Ireland to fight with the king. Both Robert and Milo returned to Ireland in 1177 and faced into a new challenge: Henry had rewarded their services with the substantial land grant of the kingdom of Cork, located far to the west of both Diarmait Mac Murchada's kingdom of Wexford and the town of Waterford. Milo and Robert were to share seven cantreds between them, and to jointly govern the city of Cork and its adjoining cantred (Kerrycurrihy). Whereas Cork city had been promised to the Normans by Diarmait Mac Carthaig in 1177 – a promise on which Diarmait had actually reneged – the grant of the seven cantreds was quite speculative, for these lands lay beyond bounds of established Norman jurisdiction.[38]

Four of the seven cantreds were granted to Milo, but the lands Robert acquired covered a larger land area. The three cantreds granted to him – Fir Maighe (the modern baronies of Fermoy and Condons and Clangibbon), Uí Liatháin (Olethan, now comprised of the modern baronies of Barrymore and Kinnatalloon) and Uí Meic Caille (the barony of Imokilly) – were to the north and east of the city, immediately contiguous with the western part of county Waterford, which remained in royal hands, and with eastern county Limerick and south-western county Tipperary, both part of Thomond, granted by Henry to Philip de Braose with whom Robert and Milo had returned to Ireland. Robert, according to custom, subdivided the lands which had been granted to him. It is Fir Maighe, Fermoy, the northernmost of his three cantreds, which interests us here [**14**].

This cantred was granted to Raymond le Gros, and he retained the eastern part, the *caput* of which was at Glanworth, while granting the western part to the fitz Hugh brothers, Alexander and Raymond, with Duncroith (Castletownroche) as *caput*.[39] The fitz Hughs first appear in Ireland as followers of Raymond le Gros, to whom they were related;[40] they were attestors to a charter concerning the le Gros lands in Leinster.[41] Their father, Hugh, was

previous pages

13   Aerial view of Bridgetown Priory from the north

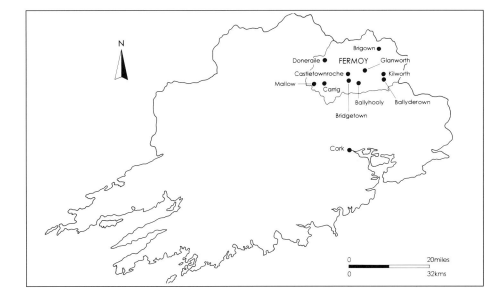

14   The medieval county of Cork and the cantred of Fermoy
Important settlements are marked within the cantred, including the *capitae* of Castletownroche and Glanworth, and Bridgetown Priory.[42]

probably the seventh son of Maurice fitz Gerald, to whom Robert fitz Stephen had granted Youghal; certainly the names Alexander and Raymond, and Griffin, the name of another brother according to the foundation charter of Bridgetown Priory (discussed below), and Nesta, also named in the charter and presumably a sister, are all associated with the fitz Geralds.[43] Raymond fitz Hugh was killed in 1185, and with that the entire western two-thirds of Fir Maighe passed onto Alexander's daughter Synolda. Her marriage eventually brought the lands into the hands of the Roches.[44]

Relations between these Anglo-Norman adventurers and their Gaelic hosts were complex. Diarmait Mac Carthaig had, like other Irish kings, sworn fealty to Henry II on his visit to Ireland in 1171, but had not acted upon it when fitz Stephen and de Cogan reached Cork; rather, Cork appears to have resisted the Norman army,[45] and needed therefore to be taken by force. In 1178 Diarmait entered into a treaty with fitz Stephen and de Cogan, surrendering to them those seven cantreds which Henry had granted to them and promising them tribute. The extent to which these cantreds were settled during the lifetimes of Robert and Milo is uncertain, but it is probable that settlement was quite insubstantial. Relative peace in the seven cantreds in the period between early 1178, when fitz Stephen and de Cogan could reasonably feel that the land was indeed theirs, and 1182, when Diarmait lead an unsuccessful revolt, and again after 1182, may be indicated on the one hand by the lack of firm evidence in the area for the earth and timber castles which were normally deployed in areas of high tension, and on the other by the evidence that some landowners could afford the luxury of building stone castles as soon as they took possession of their lands.[46] Records of ecclesiastical possessions might also be pertinent here. The early 12th-century reform of the Irish Church had resulted in the organisation of the Irish Church into dioceses, with pastoral care provided within the context of parishes. Grants of ecclesiastical revenue and the right of advowson – the right to appoint the priest – were made by the new lay patrons of parochial churches to the larger monastic institutions, according to well-established custom. With such gifts came the promise to the patrons of prayers for their salvation. Charters recording grants to monastic houses survive for the kingdom of Cork, particularly for the fitz Stephen cantreds.[47] Their very existence reflects the establishment of a parish network by the close of the 12th century, which may in turn reflect relative peace within the fiefs.

Within the diocesan estates, such grants were made by the Normans in the 1170s and 1180s to the priories of St Thomas the Martyr in Dublin and St Nicholas in Exeter, and were confirmed by the bishops of Cork.[48] The former was a house of Augustinian canons, founded in 1177, and elevated to the status of abbey of the Victorine congregation around 1192,[49] while the latter was a house of Benedictine monks, founded in 1087.[50] These priories were also recipients of grants outside the diocesan estates from fitz Stephen, de Cogan, and from their enfeoffees.[51] In 1180 Alexander and Raymond fitz Hugh, enfeoffed of the western two-thirds of Fir Maighe, gave half the revenue issuing from the church of Kilcummer and a carucate of land to St Thomas's, while Raymond le Gros, enfeoffed of the eastern third (and later to accede to Robert fitz Stephen's baronial lands in Cork), gave the other half of the revenue from the church of Kilcummer along with five carucates of land.[52]

Prior to the Anglo-Norman arrival, there had been houses of reformed monastic orders in the kingdom of Cork.[53] In the city itself, Gill Abbey, a daughter house of the Augustinian abbey of Cong, Co Mayo, was founded around 1134 by Cormac Mac Carthaig. Another house of Augustinian canons, Tullylease, was probably founded prior to the Norman arrival. In 1170, several years before the Anglo-Norman arrival in Cork, Domnall Mór Ua Briain founded a Cistercian monastery at Fermoy, and it was colonised from Inislounaght, Co Tipperary. Two years later, Diarmait Mac Carthaig founded a Cistercian monastery at Aghaminister, Co Cork, for a colony from Baltinglass, Co Wicklow; a century later the monastery moved site to Abbeymahon. The Cistercian abbey of Midleton, although founded for a colony from Monasteranenagh, Co Limerick, in 1180, may have had an Irish founder, Toirdelbach Ua Briain. Monasteries for Benedictine monks were rarely founded in Ireland, with one of only two pre-Norman houses established in the 1140s at Rosscarbery in west Cork by a community from the *Schottenklöster* in Würzburg. The Normans appear not to have been responsible for new reformed monastic

15 The base of a baptismal font
This font was of a type particularly well represented in the Kilkenny and Tipperary areas and dating from the 13th century. Its four upright colonettes and the cylindrical bowl are missing.

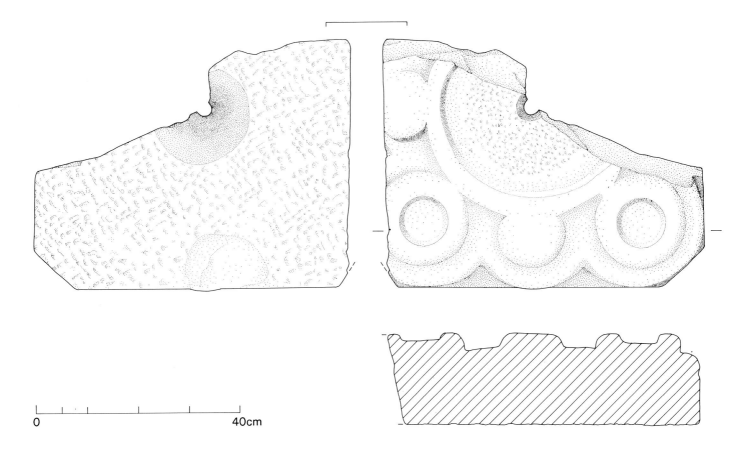

0   40cm

16 The choir of Molana Priory church
    The present ruins at Molana were built
    under the patronage of Raymond le Gros.

houses in the kingdom of Cork prior to the 13th century, apart from the establishment of two Benedictine hospitals – one in the city, the other in Youghal – and the apparent rededication and installation of monks from the Benedictine priory of St Nicholas in Exeter in the former Church of the Holy Sepulchre in Cork, a building which had been wrecked in the taking of the city by fitz Stephen and de Cogan in 1177.[54] In the 13th century, however, the number of new foundations increased, with two Cistercian abbeys (Abbeystrowry and Tracton), two Augustinian priories (Bridgetown [**13**] and Ballybeg), an Augustinian friary (Cork), two Dominican friaries (Cork and Youghal), four Franciscan friaries (Buttevant, Cork, Youghal and Timoleague), two Knights Hospitallers' preceptories (Cork and Mourne), and one nunnery (Cork).

The fact that no monastic order had a significantly greater number of new houses founded in 13th-century Cork reflects the pattern of property grants in the late 12th century; men like fitz Stephen and de Cogan, and their principal grantees, appear to have had no preference for one order over another in deciding on the destination of ecclesiastical revenues and rights of advowson. It is debatable whether many of the grants of land to monastic houses as distant from Cork as St Mary's and St Thomas's, not to mention St Nicholas's in Exeter, were envisaged as stepping stones to the actual foundation of new monasteries on those lands. This can certainly be the interpretation in the case of Milo de Cogan's grant to the Cistercian abbey of St Mary's,

Dublin, of fifteen carucates on the border between Kerrycurrihy and Kinalea.[55] The grant made to the priory of St Thomas the Martyr in Dublin by the fitz Hugh brothers in 1180 in the cantred of Fir Maighe, however, was hardly in anticipation of the foundation there of an affiliated monastery. It was nearly a quarter of a century later that Augustinian canons did settle in the fitz Hugh fief at what is now Bridgetown, and by that time Alexander was the sole patron, his brother having died in 1185. The site for Bridgetown was on the carucate given to St Thomas's in 1180, and Newtown Trim in Meath, founded in 1202, shared in its colonisation. The presence of the base of an early 13th-century baptismal font [**15**] indicates that the newly built priory must have served as a parish church.[56]

Raymond le Gros, from whom the fitz Hugh brothers were evidently enfeoffed of Fir Maighe, acted as a benefactor to the Augustinian monastery of Molana (Dair-inis), located on an island in the Blackwater estuary between Uí Meic Caille cantred and the kingdom of Decies. It is interesting to note that Molana, a pre-Norman Augustinian house, was rebuilt around the same time as Bridgetown was built [**16**].[57]

The foundation and endowments of Bridgetown Priory

The foundation of a medieval monastic house was a complex process. An invitation to a monastic order by a lord was only the beginning. Before a site could properly be said to have been founded, terms of foundation and the generosity of endowments would doubtless have been discussed at length, the proposed site would have been inspected and surveyed, the appropriate approval would have been secured, and the relevant documentation prepared.[58] Patronage of a monastery impacted directly upon a lord's enfeoffment because it tied up land and resources, and so it was a venture entered into with considerable forethought.

Contemporary records of the foundation of Bridgetown no longer survive. We depend instead on copies, made in 1290 and 1334, of the early 13th-century charter by which Alexander fitz Hugh, the priory's founder, confirmed his endowment to the monastery.[59] King John was still alive when the original charter was issued, which places the foundation before 1216, while the indication that the priory was partially colonised from SS Peter and Paul in Newtown Trim, whence it could also elect its future priors, places its foundation later than 1202.[60]

The Inspeximus (copy) of 1290 reads as follows:

The King to the Archbishops, etc., greeting. We have inspected the charter which Alexander fitz Hugh made to the canons of the house of the Blessed Mary of the Bridge in Fermoy in Ireland, in these words.

Be it known to all Christ's faithful people to whom the present writing shall come, that I Alexander fitz Hugh have given, granted and presented, and by this charter confirmed, to God and to the monastery of St Mary of the Bridge in Fermoy, and to the canons serving God there under the Rule of Saint Augustine, for the salvation of our lord John, King of England, and his ancestors and successors, and of my soul, and the souls of my father, my mother, and my wife, and of my brother Griffith, and of my ancestors and successors, that place assigned for building a monastery, and that bridge, with eight carucates of arable land, which are between the water of the Avenebeg and the land of Robert Keting in length; and between my demesne, next to my stone castle, and Avenemore, in breadth, as they have been divided and paced around and assigned from the same land; and all my land, and my grove, and the water, and all the mountains, and the pasture, which are as far as Glymbride towards Cork, between the land of Keting and the land of the nuns of Grane; and also, the five carucates of arable land upon Avenebeke: namely two by the gift of Maurice the Fleming, and three by mine, which are between the house of the aforesaid Maurice and the boundaries of the land of Calcumere; and all the water freely, as the breadth of their land may be extended, and their use and produce of all kinds.

I have also given to the same [canons] there, in the groves, all easements necessary for all kinds of use by them and their men; and a third share of my mill, and of my fishery next to my castle, without charging any custom from the canons, either for stones, or for any preparation or repair of the water mill, pond or fishery; and also all ecclesiastical benefices of all my lordship, with the tithes of mills, and hay, and fisheries, huntings, and of all things which are yearly renewed to me or my heirs; and also three burgages in Limerick, of which one is held by Nesta, the wife of Walter Corp, paying yearly for the same one half of a mark; and Siward holds the other two, paying yearly for the same one mark; and also one knight's fee in Olethan; and also another fee in Obathwen; and also a townland beside Carrig, namely that which I receive by hereditary right from my brother Remund.

I have granted all the aforesaid things to them, to have and to hold in pure, free and perpetual alms, quietly, peacefully and honourably, wholly and fully, without any service, exaction, demand, aid, tallage and geld, and without [the obligation] of keeping dogs, of making men or horses go on journeys, or military action, or on raids; and specifically from any unfree custom, and so that any alms may be given more freely and better, in wood, in plain, in ways, in paths, in waters, in ponds, grazings, pastures, moors, fisheries, huntings, mills, marshes, issues, pastures, courts, gallows, and in all other liberties and free customs which I have or can grant.

And moreover, on the death or translation of the prior, neither I nor my heirs will intrude ourselves to make any seisin of that house, or of the things pertaining to it, but the general and free disposition and government of the house and its property shall be reserved to the brethren of that place, and its prelates shall freely exercise the election; and if by chance they cannot find a suitable prior from among themselves, there may be elected by them one from the House of the Apostles Peter and Paul of Meath, or else from the house of Saint Thomas the Martyr of Dublin, from which they have taken their beginning and the form of their Order, or one from elsewhere who is of the like Order, if a sufficient and suitable one cannot be found in the aforesaid churches.

I also grant, and wish, that the said canons shall have all the betaghs of all the aforesaid lands, and their court for all disputes and pleas which arise in their lands; and those of their men, except those which happen to relate to the Crown; and the same canons shall have all manner of licence everywhere in my land, of fishing in Avenemore and in Avenebeg, in pools and outside of pools, without any interference or impediment.

It is also to be known that I, the aforesaid Alexander, and my heirs, will warrant, defend and acquit the aforesaid lands of the aforesaid canons against all secular exaction and external service; and if I and my heirs cannot warrant the said lands and pastures, waters, groves and mountains, to the aforesaid canons against all comers, we shall make in full a reasonable exchange elsewhere, in a place suitable for them, by the view of lawful men and lawful plea.

And so that this my gift and grant may remain ratified, stable and unshaken, I have considered it right for the present page to be corroborated with the defence of my seal.

Before these witnesses: Master Philip de Barre; Master William de Kantitune; Master Robert de Kantitune; Master Henry de St. Michael; Master Ris. Beket; Maurice the Fleming; Maurice de Porttrahan; and many others.[61]

And we also have granted and confirmed the aforesaid gift and grant, holding them to be approved for us and our heirs, so much as in us is, to the aforesaid canons and their successors, as the aforesaid charter reasonably witnesses.

Before these witnesses etc.
Given by our hand at Westminster, the 12th day of February [1290]

There are differences between the 1290 and 1334 versions of the charter, and indeed between the three published editions of the former,[62] but combining the evidence of the various late 13th / early 14th-century copies of the charter, it is possible to create the following composite edition (with original spellings retained) which is faithful to the original in its arrangement and language.

Alexander fitz Hugh gave, granted, and by this present charter confirmed the following lands, tenements, and hereditaments to (a) God, (b) the monastery of St Mary of the Bridge in Fermoy, and (c) the canons serving God there under the Rule of Saint Augustine, and all given for (a) the salvation of our lord John, King of England, (b) his ancestors and successors, (c) of Alexander's soul, (d) the souls of his father, his mother, and his wife, and of his brother Griffith, and of his ancestors and successors: (a) the site assigned for the monastic buildings, and the *vill de Ponte*, the castle and the bridge itself, with 8 carucates of arable land, located, divided, perambulated, and marked out between the water of the Avenebeg [Awbeg] and the land of Robert Keting, and between Alexander's demesne (beside his stone castle), and Avenemore [Blackwater]; (b) and all his land, wood, water, mountains, and pasture, located between the land of Robert Keting and the land of the nuns of Graneare and extending in the direction of Cork as far as Glymbride; (c) and those 5 carucates of arable land upon Avenebeg, two by the gift of Maurice the Fleming, and three by Alexander's own gift, which are located between the demesne (or house) of Maurice the Fleming and the boundaries of the land of Calcumere; (d) and all the water within the breadth of the land to make pools and water-courses [to dam and divert], along with their use and proceeds. Alexander also gave to the canons (e) all easements in the woods which are necessary for all kinds of uses by them and their tenants; and (f) a third share of his mill, and of his fishery next to his castle, but without charging a fee from the canons, either for stones, or for any preparation or repair of the mill, pond or fishery; also (g) all ecclesiastical benefices of all his demesne land, with the tithes of mills, hay, fisheries, huntings, and of all things which are yearly renewed to him or his heirs; also (h) three burgages in Limerick, one held by Nesta, the wife of Walter Corp, paying yearly one half-mark; and two held by Siward, paying yearly one mark; and also (i) one knight's fee in Olethan; and one knight's fee in Obathwen; and also that townland [*villatam terre*] beside Carrig which Alexander inherited from his brother Remund. Alexander granted all the above to the canons, to be held in frankalmoign [to have and to hold in pure, free and perpetual alms], quietly, peacefully and honourably, wholly and fully, free from (1a) all service, exaction, demand, aid, tallage and geld, and (1b) without the obligation of feeding servants, of keeping dogs, of maintaining men or horses, of going or sending men or horses to the army, or on raids/riding expeditions, and free from (2) any unfree custom with other liberties and privileges. All this so that any alms may be given more freely and better, in wood, in plain, in ways, in paths, in waters, in ponds, grazings, pastures, moors, fisheries, huntings, mills, marshes, issues, pastures, courts, gallows, and in all other liberties and free customs which Alexander has or can grant. On the death or translation of the prior, neither Alexander nor his heirs are to intrude to make any seisin of that house, or of the things pertaining to it; rather, (1) the general and free disposition and government of the house and its property shall be reserved to the brethren of Bridgetown, and (2) its prelates shall freely exercise the election; and (3) if a suitable prior cannot be found from among themselves, they may elect one from the SS Peter and Paul, or else from S Thomas the Martyr, from which they have taken their beginning and the form of their Order, or if one of these two churches cannot provide one, they may take one from another house of the same order. Alexander also grants and wishes that the canons shall have (1) all the *nativos* of all the aforesaid lands, and (2) their own court for all the disputes and pleas save those of the Crown which arise in their lands and among their tenants except those which happen to relate to the Crown; and (3) licence for them to fish throughout in Alexander's land in the Avenmore and in the Avenebeg, both inside and outside of pools, without any interference or impediment. Alexander and his heirs warrant, defend and acquit the aforesaid lands of the aforesaid canons against all secular exaction and foreign service; and if Alexander and his heirs cannot warrant the said lands and pastures, waters, groves and mountains, to the aforesaid canons against all comers, they will make in full a reasonable exchange elsewhere, in a place suitable for them, by the view of lawful men. And so that his gift and grant may remain ratified, stable and unshaken, he marks its with his seal. Witnesses: [Sir Philip de Prendergast],[63] Sir Philip de Barry, Sir William de Kantitune, Sir Robert de Kantitune, Sir Henry de St. Michael, Sir Rys Beket, Maurice the Fleming, and Maurice of Porttrahan, and many others. Westminster, 12th day of February.

The charter began with a statement of confirmation to God, to the monastery itself, and then to the canons there who serve God under the Rule of Saint Augustine, and of confirmation of the lands, tenements and hereditaments which have been granted to the monastic house. The grant was stated as having been made for the salvation of Lord John, of Alexander's ancestors and successors, of Alexander's soul, of the souls of his father, his mother and his wife, and of his brother Griffin, and of his ancestors and successors. The endowment was then outlined. Endowments to monastic houses such as Bridgetown were of two types, spiritual and temporal. The former was comprised of ecclesiastical income, which could involve tithes from impropriated churches and revenue from glebeland, as well as tithes from manors held by the founder. Temporalities included gifts of land, mills, fisheries, even burgages, or of the revenue issuing therefrom, as well as such rights as those of commonage or of holding fairs. The Cistercians, by contrast with the Augustinians, were actively opposed to accepting such endowments, claiming that 'churches, altar-dues, burial rights, the tithes from the work or nourishment of other men, manors, dependent labourers, land rents, revenues from ovens and mills and similar [property]' was not 'in accord with monastic purity'.[64]

The spiritualities with which Bridgetown was endowed were stated vaguely: the charter allowed to the priory 'all ecclesiastical benefices' of Alexander's demesne land. The temporalities granted by Alexander were more fully spelled out, beginning with the actual site which was assigned for the monastic buildings, as well as the bridge, the *vill de Ponte*, and the castle.

As will be seen, the priory buildings are located on a site – marshy ground along the river flood plain – which was to prove problematic, and the charter might indicate that this actual plot of ground was specified by the patron as the site on which the buildings were to be erected. It might seem unreasonable to suggest that the community would have their patron mark out on the ground exactly where he wanted the buildings, regardless of the suitability of the site, but it is not inconceivable that this was the case; at Mellifont, Co Louth, for example, the west end of the Cistercian church needed to be elevated above a crypt because the site was unsuitable, and something similar may explain in part the complex crypt system beneath the 13th-century choir of Buttevant Franciscan friary [**18**].[65]

The granting of the bridge from which Bridgetown takes its name indicates that the river Blackwater was already spanned at or near the site,[66] and also that the convent had rights to the bridge tolls. If the latter was the case, those rights had been relinquished by 1311 when the king and his bailiffs made a grant of the bridge tolls to the prior for the duration of three years.[67] The reference to a castle is intriguing. Alexander had his own castle at Duncroith (Castletownroche), so this may refer to another monument erected to protect the crossing. The *vill de Ponte* is more difficult still to assess, *vill* being one of those seemingly ambiguous medieval terms.[68] In this case it presumably referred to an actual settlement from which the convent was to receive rents.[69] This settlement was probably that which was listed as a 'market town' in 1299.[70] Whether the term 'town' conveys the form and function of a settlement *extra muros* at Bridgetown might be debated, as may the status of its inhabitants (including Adam le Fleming and John de Leye, both of whom were mentioned in 1299, or William de Staunton, named as a juror in 1313[71]). Earthworks on the high ground overlooking the priory on its south-west may indicate an actual nucleated settlement [**20**].

Alexander also donated eight carucates of arable land, located between

18　The choir of Buttevant Friary church from the south-east
Three external buttresses mark the position of the two-storeyed vault beneath the choir.

the Awbeg river and the land of Robert Keating,[72] and between Alexander's demesne (beside his stone castle) and the river Blackwater; these carucates had already been divided up, perambulated, and marked out. All the arable and pasture, wood, water and hill which Alexander possessed between the land of Robert Keating and the land of the nuns of Grange and extending in the direction of Cork as far as Glenbride was also granted. The exact geography of this part of the grant is not spelled out, suggesting that the boundaries of the land in question were well known. A further five carucates of arable land along the Awbeg, and located between the house or demesne[73] of Maurice the Fleming and the boundaries of the land of Kilcummer (on the opposite bank of Blackwater from Bridgetown), were also granted. Two of them were donated by Maurice the Fleming, the only benefactor mentioned in the charter, and three were donated by Alexander himself. Alexander also granted to the priory three burgages in Limerick, one held by Nesta, presumably a sister or niece of Alexander,[74] who was the wife of Walter Corp, for an annual rent of half a mark, and two held by Siward for an annual rent of one mark. Also granted were two knights' fees, one in Uí Liatháin and one in Obathwen [Uí Badhamhna], and a *villatam terre*, a townland, beside Carrig (east of Mallow) which he had inherited from his brother, Remund, who had died in 1182. He also gave all the bondsmen of all the lands mentioned in the charter to the priory.

Alexander also gave economic resources to the canons. He granted a third share of his demesne mill and his fishery, both located beside his castle, but he waived a fee from the canons for stones or any material needed to repair the mill, millpond or fishery. He also granted to the canons the tithes of mills, hay, fisheries, 'huntings', and of all things which belonged to tenants of Alexander or his heirs. The canons were given permission to make mill-races or water-courses and ponds on the waters running through the lands granted to them, and to use and profit from their proceeds. They were also granted access to all the easements they and their tenants required in the woods. Their principal mill was placed immediately south of the priory, and was served by a now-dry mill-race which cut off the bend of the river, and along which were three stone sluice gates, only one of which survives, overgrown and with its arch destroyed. The canons were also granted the entitlement to hold their own court for all the disputes and pleas which arose in their lands and among their tenants, save those of the Crown.

On the death or translation of the prior, Alexander guaranteed that neither he nor his heirs were to intrude to make any claim on the house, or on the chattels which belonged to it. Instead, the disposition and government of the house and its property was reserved to the brethren of Bridgetown, with a new prior to be elected by its prelates, and in the event of them not being able to find a suitable prior from among themselves, they were empowered to elect one from the SS Peter and Paul in Newtown Trim [**21**], or else from the Abbey of St Thomas the Martyr, or if one of these two churches could not provide

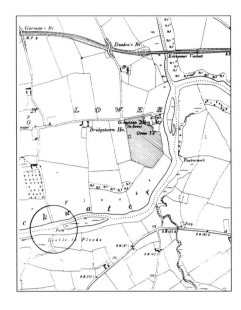

19　Bridgetown Priory location map
The ford over the Blackwater (ringed) probably marks the site of the bridge. A small roadway runs towards it from the north. Earthworks are located in the area marked with diagonal shading. No earthworks have survived deep ploughing in the fields to the west and south-west.

20　Earthworks at Bridgetown Priory
The large field to the south-west of the buildings contains earthworks. Contour mapping of the entire field (top left) reveals a north-south arrangement of large banks and terraces. In the southern half of the field (top right) are the traces of what may have been a very substantial square building along the west side of the field, and this is clearly represented in a three-dimensional model (bottom).

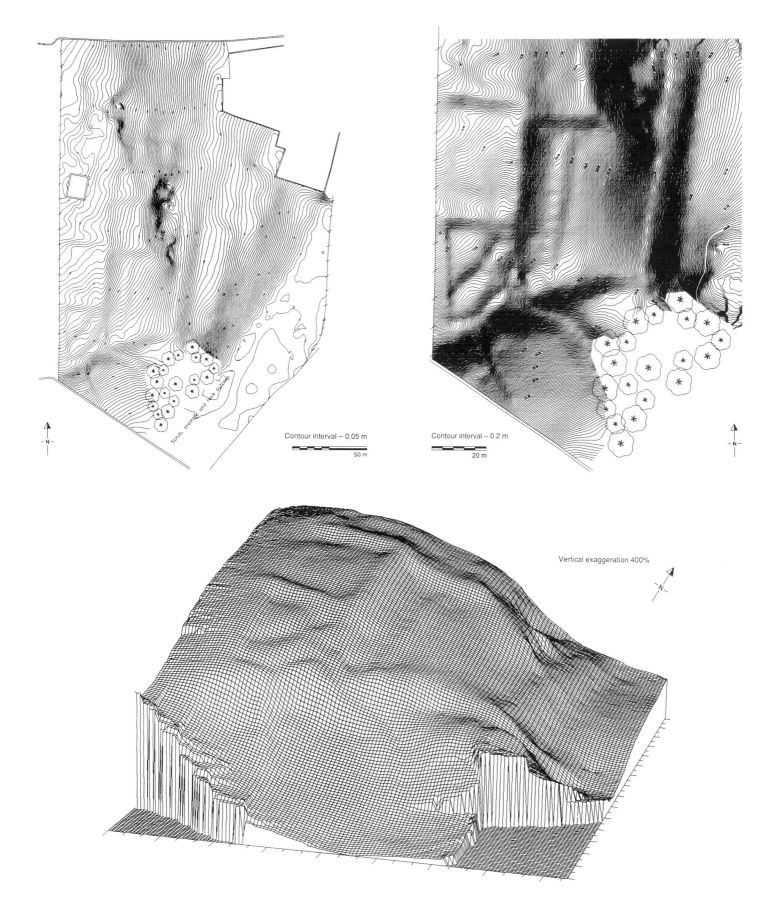

Contour interval – 0.05 m

50 m

Contour interval – 0.2 m

20 m

Scrub, bramble and flint outcrop

Vertical exaggeration 400%

39

one, they were empowered to take one from another house of the same order.[75] Although it was not stated, Alexander would probably have reserved certain rights of patronage for himself, in the matter of granting a licence for an election, and in confirming the choice of new prior.[76] Alexander did expressly guarantee on his behalf and on behalf of his heirs that the lands of the canons would be protected against all secular exaction and external service, and he promised that if lands and pastures, waters, groves and mountains could not be warranted against all comers, then a new location would be made available for the canons.

The witnesses to the charter listed included Sir Philip de Prendergast,[77] Sir Philip de Barry,[78] Sirs William and Robert de Kantitune,[79] Sir Henry de St Michael, Sir Rys Beket,[80] Maurice the Fleming, and Maurice of Porttrahan.

By this charter Alexander committed his heirs to the protection of the monastery's possessions and rights, as was customary,[81] with the grant outlined in the charter to be held in frankalmoign, or 'free alms' tenure, and with provision for further alms to be donated to the monastery:

> I have granted all the aforesaid things to them, to have and to hold in pure, free and perpetual alms, quietly, peacefully and honourably, wholly and fully, without any service, exaction, demand, aid, tallage and geld, and without [the obligation] of feeding servants keeping dogs, of making men or horses go on journeys, or sending them to the army, or on raids; and specifically from any unfree custom, and so that any alms may be given more freely and better, in wood, in plain, in ways, in paths, in waters, in ponds, grazings, pastures, moors, fisheries, huntings, mills, marshes, issues, pastures, courts, gallows, and in all other liberties and free customs which I have or can grant.

The grant to the monastery of possessions in 'pure, free and perpetual alms' follows the contemporary convention.[82] The giving of possessions as 'alms' established a peculiar tenurial relationship between the grantor and the grantee: land grants within the secular domain were reciprocated with services, sometimes of a military nature, but in the case of grants to monastic houses the return on the gift was the anticipation that the grant would garner salvation for the soul of the deceased, either directly through the community's prayers, or, indeed, through their own giving of alms to the poor. The giving of alms to Bridgetown in perpetuity, combined with the provision in the charter for freedom from exaction so that alms may be given to the community by future benefactors, addressed directly the realisation that prayers were as necessary for the salvation of souls after death as before it.[83] Possessions granted and held as 'free alms' would fall within the jurisdiction of ecclesiastical courts in cases of dispute. Whether it was the spiritualities or temporalities of a monastery, or both, which were held by 'free alm' or frankalmoign, is a moot point, but in the 12th century, ecclesiastical – or rather, episcopal – authority claimed jurisdiction over all the property anyway.[84]

In the last third of the century, during the reign of Henry II (a noted

21 Newtown Trim, looking eastwards
    along the river Boyne
    The Priory of St John the Baptist, a
    13th-century hospital and church run by
    the Fratres Cruciferi ('crutched friars'),
    stands beside a medieval bridge a little
    downriver.

legal reformer), it became necessary for a royal writ to be issued in order for the possession of land to be challenged, either by a lord or a tenant, and even though royal writs could be easily purchased [85] and presented at a seigniorial or ecclesiastical court, there was certainly an increasing tendency for disputes concerning monastic possessions to be brought before the royal court where they could be resolved most speedily. [86] In the case of Bridgetown, the circumstance in which the 1290 Inspeximus seems to have been issued was an application by the community to the king for the reaffirmation of its rights after previous priors had alienated property without consent. [87] Indeed, earlier in 1255 the King ruled in favour of the prior in a dispute concerning two carucates. [88] Increasing royal involvement in the adjudication of disputes regarding possessions contributed to a standardisation of the format and legal terminology of charters after the turn of the 13th century. Thus the Bridgetown charter opened with King John named first among those whose souls were likely to profit by the grant. [89] The royal imprimatur was also added to the donor's own guarantee that the possessions would be held in perpetuity, unless of course the charter contained a provision which was deemed contrary to common law, as was the case with the canons' request in 1289 that their poor tenants be spared jury service. By the end of the 13th century, land coming into the possession of churches was no longer accepted as 'free alms' but was subjected to the rigours of tenurial law, [90] and so, when Prior Henry acquired in fee a rent of 50s in Bridgetown in 1302, it was seized from him and taken into the king's hands because it was done contrary to the Statute of Mortmain and without licence. Henry was pardoned of this transgression and paid a fine of £10 in order to recover this rent.[91]

––––––––

The primary source of wealth for a monastery such as Bridgetown would have been the patron's own endowment, but other benefactors were welcome.[92] Only one appears, however, to have made a grant to Bridgetown at its foundation: Maurice the Fleming, the nephew of Alexander fitz Hugh and a witness to the original charter. Maurice's grant of two carucates is given in the charter, but there was also a separate charter of confirmation[93] of a grant by him, in 'pure, free and perpetual alms', to the priory of the ecclesiastical benefices in his tenement of Fermoy, and of the two ploughlands of land which are described as next to the Awbeg in 'Glinnemanahac' and in 'Cnokenynog'. This grant was witnessed by Alexander fitz Hugh himself, along with Walter de Cauntetune, Philip de Barry (who also witnessed Bridgetown's foundation charter), Walter Magner, Hamo Beket, Philip Beket, Thomas de Cantenune, Simon, his brother, and others unnamed. By the time of the first Inspeximus of 1290, Bridgetown had doubtless drawn other benefactors,[94] and the priory's comparative health – a valuation of £40 in the ecclesiastical taxation of Nicholas IV in 1291 – owes something to acts of benefaction during the 13th century, but none was mentioned in the Inspeximus. It was not the purpose of an Inspeximus to update the primary document, and in any case the 1289 request of the community for the king's assistance in restoring what had been unlawfully alienated by previous priors probably referred to gifts which were made to the monastery after Alexander's original charter was drawn up, and which do not therefore appear in the Inspeximus. Indeed, Bridgetown was receiving tithes from the church Maurice had built in Carrig, located on the east side of Mallow, a matter which was disputed in 1307.[95] Among the priory's other, erstwhile possessions, recorded in Papal transactions in the late Middle Ages, were the churches of Ballyhay, Kilmacdonagh, Shandrum, Ballyhay, Ballyhooly, Kyllahy and Littir,[96] to which early 17th-century sources can add others.[97]

–––––

The priorship of Bridgetown

The priors of Bridgetown remain largely unknown to us. For the first two centuries of the monastery's life, we know of priors mainly by their first names. William, the only prior named in the 13th century, was promoted to the see of Cloyne in 1226.[98] Remaining unnamed is the prior, or the priors, who habitually incurred fines for trespass in the 1280s: five times between 1285 and 1288 a fine of 20s was levied,[99] but once, in 1285, the fine was 106s 8d.[100] In 1302, a Brother Robert le Erseekene of the priory was recorded as having actually paid a fine of 20s for trespass.[101] This Brother Robert may have been a prior. In the same year[102] the priorship was recorded as belonging to a Henry;[103] he was also named as prior in 1307.[104] In 1322, William, Archbishop of Cashel, having already incurred excommunication himself, confirmed Thomas as prior-elect of Bridgetown, who had also been excommunicated.[105] In 1370 the prior was William,[106] in 1375 it was Thomas,[107] in 1376 it was Richard Caveton,[108] the first prior whose full name we know, and in 1403 it was Brother Bartholomew.[109]

For the first three-quarters of the 15th century no priors are mentioned. Then, starting in 1470, the priory entered into a long phase in which there appears to be considerable dispute about the possession of the priorship. The condition of the charter had been that the community elected its head from among its own number, and failing that, from one of the other houses of the order, and this process may have yielded the priors mentioned above. But, as the papal correspondence indicates, the priory had become void by the later 1400s at least, and its collation had lapsed to the apostolic see, and the Pope, while recognising that the priory was elective, took control of appointments.

Between about 1470 and 1480, the priory was in the possession of Dermit Oleyni, a canon, but he had no title to it. In 1480, the Pope, on learning that the priory had been void for some time,[110] and that its collation had therefore lapsed to the apostolic see, ordered that Philip Roche, a dean of Cloyne, was to be received as a canon of the community and, pending an inquiry by the papal mandatories into Oleyni's retention of the priory, be granted the priorship in 1480.[111] Four years later, Philip was confirmed as the prior of Bridgetown but had not yet taken possession of it.[112] In 1485-86, with Phillip Roche still not in possession, a mandate was issued to grant the priorship to Nicholas, a Cistercian and the bishop of Lismore and Waterford, who claimed that both Dermit Oleyni and Philip Roche had in turn claimed the priorship on the pretext of collations made to them.[113] Nicholas himself, 'who behaves as bishop of Waterford and Lismore', was certainly not free of blemish: the same allegation that the priorship was obtained by the same false means was levied against him in 1488-89.[114] It was ordained, therefore, that Nicholas would be replaced by Maurice Odahyll, a secular canon of Emly, who revealed himself to be anxious to serve at Bridgetown under the regular habit. Maurice's enthusiasm was rewarded with permission to take possession

22 Bridgetown Priory
    from the north-west
    The tower, inserted into the west end of
    the church in the late Middle Ages,
    continued to be used for domestic
    purposes after the monastic community
    had left Bridgetown. A small brick-lined
    oven was inserted into it in the 17th
    century.

23 The Refectory
    viewed from the east
    The western end of the 13th-century
    refectory was substantially altered in the
    post-medieval period. The gable of the
    refectory was rebuilt, complete with
    musket loops for protection.

of the priory even before being professed a regular canon.[115] In 1492 Maurice died; he had been involved in litigation against a rival for the priorship, and although he was successful, he died before he could take possession of the priory, and so Nicholas retained possession. Again pending inquiry, the Pope authorised that Maurice Odahyll be replaced by Conrad Roche, a canon of Molana, who then promptly disappears from the Bridgetown record.[116]

The rival against whom Maurice Odahyll had fought in the courts may have been Philip Roche, whose resignation from a priorship of which he had never taken possession was recorded in 1493.[117] Equally, it may have been Nicholas himself who continued to detain the priory during Maurice's unsuccessful priorship, and who was to become involved in a similar litigation [118] over the priory with the man named as Philip's successor, Henry Roche, a brother of the Hospital of St John.[119] In order to acquire the priorship, Henry, the preceptor of Mourne,[120] had first to be entered into the order, but before his profession, his successor at Mourne, Donatus, drew the Pope's attention to errors in official letters regarding the collation of Mourne, apparently out of concern that his own succession would be affected.[121] Henry had also relaxed habits of continence at Mourne, daring to publicly have a concubine, and to have issue by her, and to alienate moveable goods of the preceptory. The Pope ruled, not unnaturally, that Henry was unworthy of the preceptory.[122] Although it is not recorded, he presumably considered Henry unworthy of Bridgetown also, but notwithstanding the lawsuit between Henry and Nicholas, the Pope instead elected in 1497 that James Walsh, a canon of Bridgetown, was to become prior.[123] Curiously, he was the first canon of the house we know to have become prior for more than half a century. Half a century later, at the Dissolution of the monasteries, the prior was named as William Walsh.[124] His residence within the monastery may well have been the tower attached to the south side of the precinct by one his predecessors in the late 15th century [**24**].

Remarkably, then, not only was the Pope unable to provide priors from within the community in the later 15th century, but he also had difficulty finding suitable canons regular. It is probable that the problem of finding persons 'sufficient and suitable' to the task, as the original charter put it, emerged long before it comes to our attention in the later 1400s,[125] and possibly remained the situation in the early 1500s. References to three different priors of Bridgetown in the 1370s – William, Thomas and Richard Caveton – represents something of a bonanza of information in the middle of a century generally lacking illumination, but it may well reflect a quick and unhealthy turnover of priors, after which there is documentary silence for the best part of another century. At its peak in the 13th and early 14th centuries, Bridgetown may well have had a respectable community size,[126] but the difficulty which was experienced in filling the priorship in the late 1400s suggests that the size of the Bridgetown community had contracted greatly by then. Yet, between 1449 and 1504 there were no less than twenty-one occasions on which priors (unnamed, alas) of Bridgetown acted as papal mandatories.[127] Perhaps the power to execute papal mandates was deliberately bestowed on the priorship of Bridgetown, not so much as a bait to worthy candidates, but as a means of simply keeping an active priorship at a time when the monastery may have been struggling to survive. Yet, late medieval alterations to the priory [**22**] do not suggest poverty, although parts of the priory may have needed rebuilding [**23**] once it passed into secular hands in the late 16th and 17th centuries.

———

24 The Prior's Tower

In the 12th century an abbot or prior was expected to sleep with the rest of the community in the common dormitory, but from the 13th century onwards, the heads of the communities gradually acquired their own private space, sometimes (though not at Bridgetown) a detached lodging comprised of a complex of rooms including a chapel, a hall, and guest accommodation.

✠ 3

The Monastic Rule and the Mason's Ruler

The layout and building history of Bridgetown Priory

CHURCHES WERE THE CANVASES ON WHICH NEW ARCHITECTURAL AESTHETICS and advances in technology were most frequently displayed in the Middle Ages, but all the principal elements of their design – layout, scale, symbolism – were conditioned primarily by the need to create an appropriate environment for a broad spectrum of liturgical activity.[128] From the time that the concept of church-building emerged in a complex interplay of two late Antique architectural forms – the *basilica* (a hall) and the *memoria* (a burial room) – the design of churches has remained connected umbilically to liturgical practices. Churches are machines for liturgy. This is as true of small parochial churches as it is of larger abbey and cathedral churches. Members of the medieval laity were required by obligation to be present in their church no more often than is the case today. Sunday, then as now, was the day of the Mass, the principal liturgical rite.

The interior space of a medieval church was hierarchical. At a macroscale, it was divided into two parts: the main liturgical area to the east and the area for congregation to the west. In parish churches and smaller chapels such a bipartite division was marked by a dividing wall perforated by an arch (the chancel arch) or, where the interior of a church was structurally undifferentiated, a wooden screen or rail. In larger cathedral and monastic churches there were micro-scale subdivisions, particularly in the eastern arm of the church.[129] The basic subdivision here was between the presbytery or sanctuary in which the high altar was located and the choir, located to its west, where the community sat facing each other across the floor. There were two rows of stalls against the side walls, with junior brethren sitting at the front and more senior brethren behind. For members of monastic communities, a quarter of the day or more could be spent in the eastern part of the church participating in the Mass and in that cycle of sung prayer, based on the psalms, which constituted the Divine Office. The monastic day began before dawn with Matins and Lauds, followed by Prime and Terce during the morning, Sext and None in the early afternoon, and Vespers and Compline in the later afternoon. Between

Prime and Terce was the first Mass of the day, and between Terce and Sext the second, more important, Mass.[130]

Medieval monasteries, of which the churches were but one part, generally possessed ground plans which articulated both the coherence of the communities within and the separation of those communities from the world beyond. In the earliest stratum of monasticism it was the boundary wall within which the church and other monastic buildings were placed which created this exclusiveness, as in early medieval Ireland, where the boundary wall usually enclosed a circular area. Alternatively, there was the claustral plan, in which all the buildings of the monastery, including the church, were conjoined and looked inwards on a central courtyard or cloister (*claustrum*). This layout had developed from complex sources before the early 9th century when it appears fully formed on the so-called Plan of St Gall, a manuscript ground plan of a Carolingian monastery which was never actually built.[131] It became the dominant plan type used in medieval Europe, being used among communities following, at first, the Rule of St Benedict and, after the late 11th century, the Rule of St Augustine.[132] Hitched to the belt of reformed monasticism, the claustral plan transcended boundaries of time and space. Whether it was the most efficient layout available to the orders of the mid-11th century and later was not an issue which they debated; it worked perfectly well, and it did have the imprimatur of tradition behind it. The Rule of St Augustine may have encouraged à la carte monasticism, but the claustral plan was no less useful here than among other orders, even if Augustinian communities could function as effectively without it.

The plan of Bridgetown Priory

In the claustral plan, the church occupied one side (normally the north side) of the square or rectangular courtyard, with the other activities of the monastery taking place within the interconnected buildings or suites of rooms around the other three sides. Time wasted moving between different parts of a claustral monastery was minimised by the judicious placement of functions within the spaces available; for example, the community's dormitory was always adjacent to the east of the church at upper-storey level on the east side of the cloister, thus shortening the trip from the bed to the choir. Bridgetown, like all substantial monasteries in the Norman world, was laid out to the claustral plan [**25**, **26**], and even though it is curiously H-shaped due to the lack of a west range and to the projection eastwards of the south range, the functions of each part can be identified with some confidence [**27**], as can their chronology [**28**].

In common with most medieval Irish buildings, Bridgetown's walls are

previous pages

25   Aerial view of Bridgetown Priory from the south

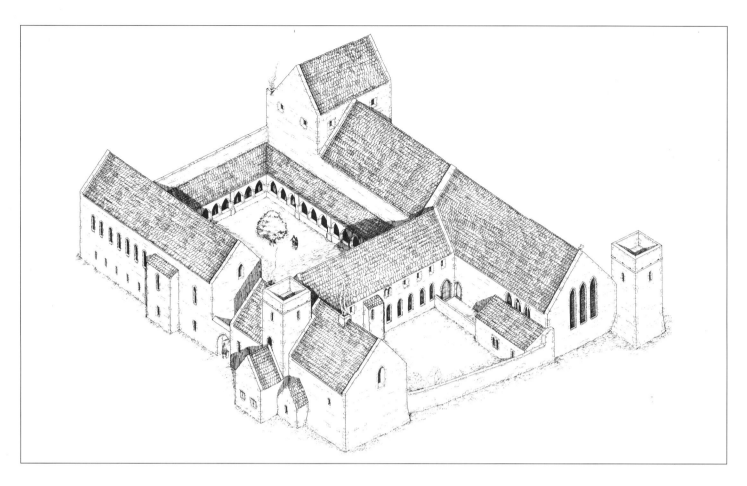

26 Reconstruction drawing of
Bridgetown Priory as it may have
appeared in the late Middle Ages
(David Hill, John Harrison & Associates)

27 Ground plan of Bridgetown Priory
showing the principal functions of
different parts of the complex
Features discovered by Dermot Twohig –
wall foundations and dug pits – are
shown in black. The pits were only found
inside the eastern part of the refectory
undercroft.

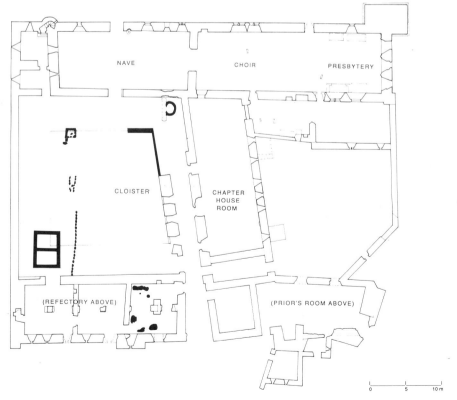

NAVE   CHOIR   PRESBYTERY

CLOISTER   CHAPTER
HOUSE
ROOM

(REFECTORY ABOVE)   (PRIOR'S ROOM ABOVE)

0   5   10 m

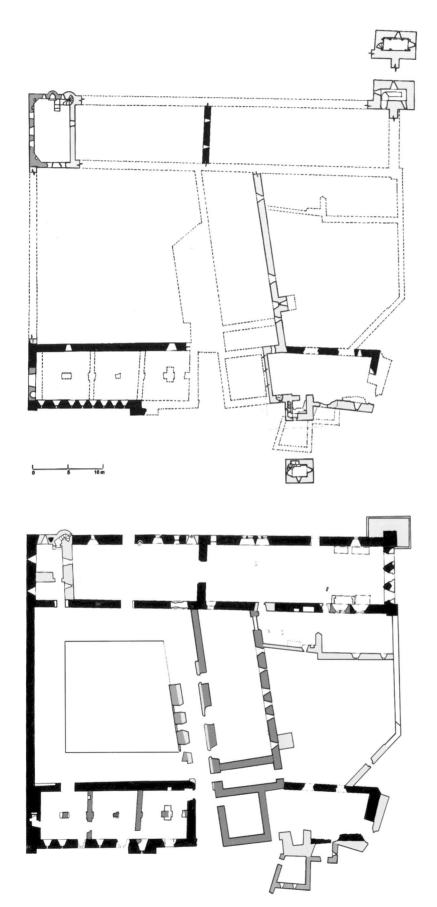

28 The principal phases of
    construction at Bridgetown Priory
    (top) upper level plans
    (bottom) ground level plan

■ early 13th century

■ later 13th century

□ late Medieval

■ 17th century ?

29 *Ex situ* sculpture, apparently
    unfinished, from Bridgetown Priory
    These fragments, together with the stone
    head [**12**], were found by Dermot
    Twohig in the excavation of the eastern
    part of the refectory. One fragment (B)
    has a row of small crosses, apparently an
    abandoned attempt at making dog-tooth
    ornament (a typical 13th-century
    decorative device), while another
    fragment appears to represent a stone
    cranium (C) complete with eye sockets
    and small projecting dots representing
    eyes. All the fragments are fashioned in
    oolithic limestone. [see also page 54]

of largely uncoursed, limestone rubble construction. Indeed, one of the difficulties of establishing the chronology of many Irish buildings is the homogeneity of fabric, even after alterations have been made. The quality of construction at Bridgetown, however, was remarkably poor from the outset, and in the late Middle Ages it saw little improvement. Where it is possible to examine the nature of the fabric closely, the walls appear to have hollow cores. Indeed, the fact that parts of the medieval walling – particularly the south side of the refectory – still stand is remarkable.

Local sandstones of differing colour and texture were used for sculptural detail in the priory in the 13th and early 14th centuries, as was normal in Ireland, with harder limestones used for details in the late Middle Ages. Also in the earlier period, oolithic limestone was imported from overseas, probably from south-west England,[133] for architectural sculpture, but the only extant sculptures in that material were recovered *ex situ* from archaeological deposits inside the refectory, and some of them seem to have been left unfinished [**12**, **29**].

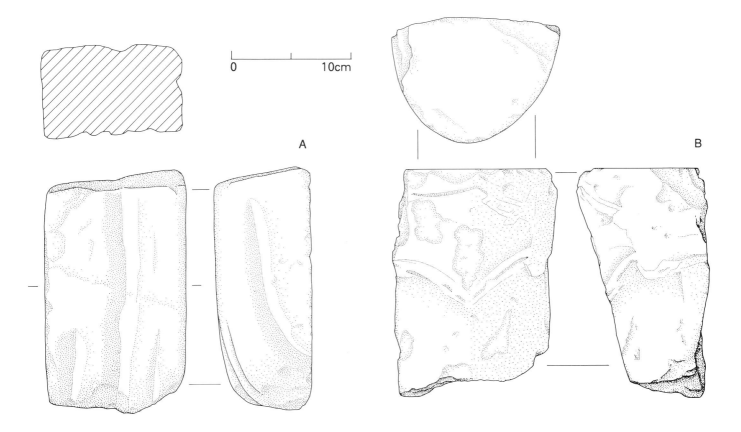

0   10cm

A

B

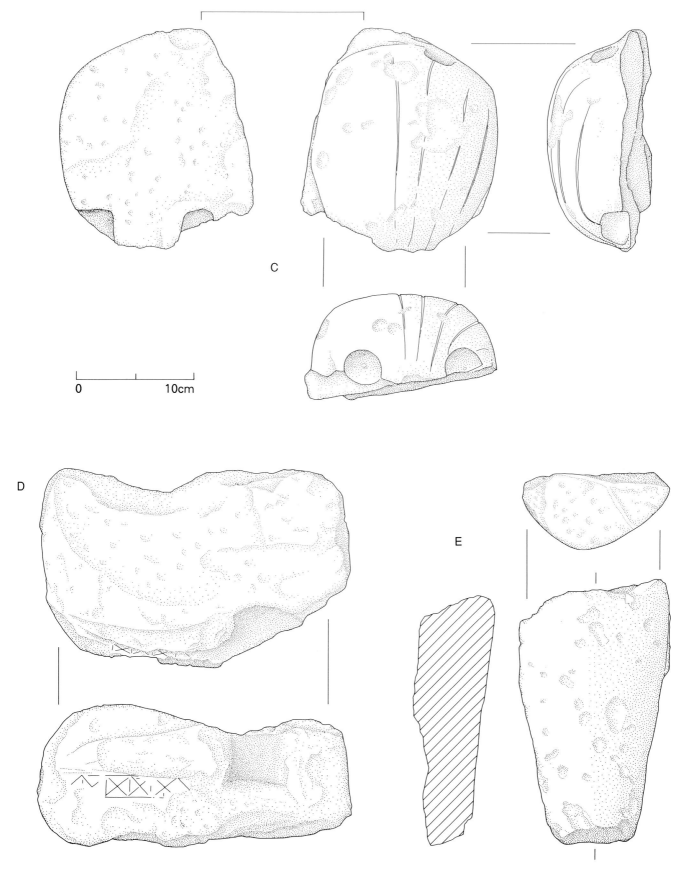

Bridgetown Priory Church

The church takes up almost the entire north side of the monastic precinct [**30, 147**]. Internally 7.95m wide, it is divided by a cross-wall into a nave, 22.7m long, on the west side, and a choir, 25.12m long, on the east. At the west end of the church is a rectangular tower, equal in width to the church and with its north and south walls carrying on the lines of the side walls of the church. Another rectangular tower projects from the external north-east corner of the choir; a solid masonry pilaster occupies the south-east corner.

The Nave

The church is entered through an archway – rebuilt with a segmental arch, 190cm wide and of unknown original width – at the west end of the north wall. A stoup is built into the interior wall of the church immediately east of this entrance. On the south wall opposite is another equally simple segmental-arched entranceway, 178cm wide, opening into the cloister. Photographs taken by Dermot Twohig in the late 1970s show this much as it is today, with a segmental pointed arch and horizontal slots running across the jambs on

29   *Ex situ* sculpture from Bridgetown Priory [see caption page 53]

30   Bridgetown Priory from the north

each side. A third doorway at the east end of the south wall of the nave was originally a processional doorway giving access to the interior of the church from the eastern cloister ambulatory and ultimately from the exterior south side of the entire complex. Originally about 180cm wide, nothing survives of the actual doorway today except a few unmoulded voussoirs on the interior and exterior, probably from a rubble relieving arch above original carved stonework, and what appears to be part of the reveal of the west side of the opening. The space which the doorway formerly occupied has been blocked since early this century if not earlier.

The nave is lit by four windows in the north wall and by two small windows high up in the partition wall. The window west of the entrance has its arch and jambs restored, but the width of its splay indicates that it was always a single light. The window immediately east of the entranceway was a twin-light set in a segmental-arched embrasure; the moulded stones of the opening are externally rebated and have both internal and external chamfers, with the internal chamfers flush with the internal splays. Most of the sill stone, mullion stones and arch stones are missing. Set in a splay of similar size, albeit with a segmental pointed roof, is the window beside the partition wall. The opening

31   The interior of the nave, looking eastwards to the partition wall

is mullioned, but the stones of which it is comprised are clearly reused from elsewhere in the complex. Between these two windows, and positioned much lower in the wall, is a blocked window, originally double-splayed.

The partition wall [**31**], 115cm thick, survives to nearly its original height and is penetrated by a comparatively small arch, 280cm wide, two small windows and six symmetrically positioned putlog holes. The voussoirs are missing from both sides of the rebuilt, bluntly pointed arch, and only a few chamfered stones survive on the west side of the rebuilt jambs. The two windows are long and rectangular with plain lintels and jambs, and are set in round-arched splays which open onto the nave. Identical windows appear in the wall at the east end of the nave of St Mary's church, Youghal, Co Cork. The partition wall has two setbacks in thickness where it faces onto the nave; one of these is directly above the arch, and the other above the windows.

The west tower [**22**] has two storeys, and rises high above the level of both the cloister and the church. Originally built in the late Middle Ages and inserted into the west end of the nave, its upper level appears to have been considerably remodelled in the 16th or, more likely, the 17th century, and in recent years it has seen extensive repairs. It is entered today through a rebuilt doorway in the cloister. The lower storey is divided by a cross-wall running west-east into two vaulted rooms, the vaults running at 90° to each other. The partition and vaults are additions, and the insertion of the latter necessitated the blocking of two small windows in the west wall of the tower. The stair to the upper storey rises in a small, roughly semi-cylindrical turret projecting from the north-east corner. The second storey has large rectangular windows (all of them recent, although they possibly reflect a late-medieval or early modern scheme), two chimneys in the north-west and south-west corners, tall gables to the north and south, and an oven in the north wall with a smoke hole contained within a small corbelled projection on the exterior wall.

The Choir and Lady Chapel

The long choir measures 7.95m by 25.12m internally [**32**]. The exterior is flanked at the north-east corner by a tower, and at the opposite corner by a buttress [**33**]. The tower is a late-medieval addition. Its lower stages were originally entered from the choir through a doorway, the exact nature of which is now lost to us through unsympathetic repair. The tower can now only be entered at an upper-storey level through a second doorway – a chamfered round arch with plain jambs – high up on the choir wall. A small head is carved on the jamb stone of the uppermost window in the north wall of the tower.

Two small doorways, placed opposite each other, originally opened off the interior west end of the choir, one giving access to the exterior north side of the complex, the other (the larger of the two) to the priory's east range. The latter was probably used for entering the church from the dormitory, which would have occupied the entire upper storey of the east range. The only details we have of the form of these doorways are some plain jamb stones still *in situ* in the southern doorway, and fragments of the arch over the lobby of the northern doorway. Two other doorways open into the east end of the choir, one from the small chapel – identified here as a Lady chapel – on the south side of the choir, and the other from the smaller walled enclosure beside it to the west. The latter doorway is at the junction of the external walls of the choir and east range, but is cut through by the choir wall in such a way that it is overlapped by the wall of the east range. A hanging eye and one of the chamfered jambs are preserved here. An older blocked doorway is evident immediately to the east. Of the other doorway, only the east side has survived reconstruction. Here some chamfered jamb stones are still *in situ* and their dressing suggests a late-medieval date. The arch is destroyed, but part of it was still extant early this century [**44**].

All of the interior east wall, except for about 70cm at each side, is taken up with the great three-light east window [**32**, **33**, **126**]. There is clear evidence of extensive rebuilding: the centre of the wall below the window is rebuilt, and virtually all of the outer fabric at the upper level – including the windows – represents a second, later, phase of rebuilding. Only the central splay has a complete window in it today. A simple traceried affair contained within a pointed frame, this is a round-headed twin-light with a transom and a symmetrical pattern of three mouchettes. It is executed in limestone and is chamfered on both sides, with the external chamfers being wider. It might be assigned to the end of the 15th century. Only fragments of chamfered jambs, also in limestone and almost certainly of the same late date, survive of the two side windows. The internal splays, which are early 13th-century works, are bordered by bowtell mouldings with fillets, flanked by narrow chamfers, all executed in red sandstone [**35**]. These are no longer continuous around the splays, but are interrupted by plainly dressed stones, inserted at some stage in the wall's history. The rear arches are destroyed in all three cases.

The splays were also bordered originally by thin, semi-detached shafts, creating an effect which would not have been dissimilar to that at St Mary's, New Ross, Co Wexford [**36**]. A string-course, semi-cylindrical in section and with a fillet, runs along the internal wall-faces of the choir at the level of the bases of the window splays, ending close to the partition wall. It might have served to separate the choir stalls from the fenestration. At both ends of the east wall, the string-course rises step-like for 20cm [**32**] to form the sill of the east window. Only the bases of these survive *in situ*; each is semi-circular and is comprised of a torus moulding above a simple chamfer. These bases in their turn stand on semi-circular projections of the string-course, while beneath those projections are tapering corbels (one of them destroyed) which terminate in twisting leaf motifs [**34**]. None of the capitals associated with these shafts is *in situ*, and none of the stones from the actual 13th-century window openings (as distinct from the splays) is known to survive.

33
34   35   opposite

33   The exterior east wall of the choir
     Mining of the base of the tower to the
     right reveals that it concealed a buttress
     similar to that on the opposite corner.

34   A corbel with a plant terminal on
     the east window at Bridgetown

35   Plan of the east window
     The rear responds and wide splays are
     original 13th-century features; the
     narrow lights are late medieval.

36   The east window of St Mary's
     parish church, New Ross,
     Co Wexford
     Even without vaulting, but with a
     wooden roof instead, a triple-light east
     window – taking up the full width of the
     wall and with the central light a little
     higher than the side lights – was a highly
     effective design.

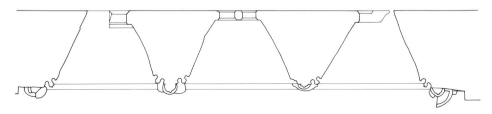

Four bluntly pointed, externally chamfered and rebated windows provided the choir with light from the north side. The two westernmost windows of the choir were twin-lights, although of the two only that to the west retains its mullions and pointed arches. The splays have surrounds of engaged shafts with fillets, and moulded bases which are now too denuded for close stylistic analysis. The two other windows are single-lights; the one which is more or less in the centre of the wall has been broken through and facilitates the stile which gives access to the church interior. It preserves an internal hood moulding with decorated stops [**79**].

On the opposite wall, clustered near to its east end, were three windows, all of them twin-lights, but only the middle one survives as such. This particular window, which may be assigned to *c.*1300, has a pair of trefoils, the spandrels of which are perforated, and a quatrefoil, grooved to take glass, above the mullion [**39**, **40**]. This type of window belongs within the tradition of the English Decorated style [**37**, **38**].[134] Of the other two windows, only the external jambs – chamfered and rebated – survive *in situ*, although among the *ex situ* stones from the site are fragments of cusps from what appears to have been another Decorated window. Internally, the jambs of the splays of both the extant Decorated window and the window adjoining it on the west [**44**]

37 Windows at Tintern Abbey, Monmouthshire, in the Decorated style

38 Panels from the façade at Tintern Abbey, Monmouthshire, in the Decorated style

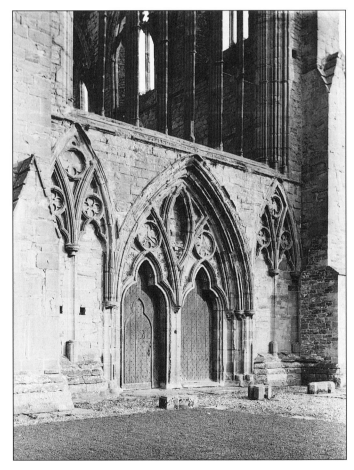

39 Window at Bridgetown Priory in
the Decorated style
The window in the south wall of the
choir is viewed here from the south, with
the Lady chapel in the foreground

have double-banded shafts with fillets, and collared capitals and bases, but
their rear-arches have been rebuilt. The internal jambs of the other window in
the south wall – the easternmost of the three – have plainly dressed stone. A
springer with a socket for a wooden strut is virtually all that survives of the
arch. Built into the rebuilt wall beneath this window is a small base, possibly
from the eastern shaft of the splay of the twin-light window.

Founders and patrons of monastic churches assumed that they would
be allowed burial in the choirs of the churches which they had endowed. As
we have seen in the discussion of the foundation charter above, this was part
of the deal of patronage; burial under the eyes of priors and canons carried
with it the promise of endless prayers after death. The great canopied tomb
against the south wall of the Bridgetown choir [**40**, **44**] could mark the burial
place of the priory's founder, Alexander fitz Hugh, but the tomb itself is no
older than late 14th century. The inverted fish suggests that the tomb was
intended for a Roche,[135] and so it seems more likely that here was the burial
place of a later benefactor of that family. Certainly the other tombs in the choir
belong to late-medieval benefactors [**41**, **42**, **43**]. A tomb marked 'Founder's
Tomb' is indicated in the centre of the east end of the choir in Horgan's plan
of the site [**4**], but that plan is so inaccurate that this cannot be trusted.

Outside the choir on the east side are two walled enclosures, both
added in the late Middle Ages and both originally roofed. That to the east

63

40 42
41 43

40 Roche tomb and twin-light
    Decorated style window in the
    south wall of the choir

41 Late 15th or early 16th-century
    grave slab in the choir showing an
    unusual pattern of tracery

42 Part of the late 15th or early
    16th-century grave slab built into
    the Roche tomb

43 Late 15th or early 16th-century
    grave slab in the choir

opposite
44 The Roche tomb, adjacent door
    and 13th-century window as they
    appeared in the early 20th century

45 The Lady chapel,
looking eastwards

might be identified as a Lady chapel. Chapels in this position were commonly dedicated to the Blessed Virgin Mary and were the scenes of masses in her honour. The date of the chapel is uncertain. Its two extant windows, both in the south wall, are round-arched and cut in limestone [141], suggesting an early 16th-century date. The doorway which leads into this small chapel from the church is conceivably older [44].

The adjacent 'enclosure' on the west side [47] was also entered through a late-medieval doorway from the church; the outline of an older, blocked doorway is visible in the wall to the east. This was certainly a burial chapel. Within it is a fine late 13th-century tomb slab with chamfered edges and a cross in quatrefoil, which now stands upright in the ground [47], an altar tomb of Theobald Roche dated 1634 [46], and a low segmental-arched tomb recess in the external south wall of the church.

46 Late 13th-century tomb slab
This early 20th-century photograph shows medieval fabric which no longer survives on the south side of the choir to the east of the Lady chapel: two arched recesses from which dressed stone has clearly been robbed, a chamfered corbel in the wall above the arches, and in the wall behind, the trace of a sloping roof and what seems to be a twin-light window. The tomb beneath the two arched recesses is still *in situ*. Its long side panel is inscribed with the name Theobald Roche, and the date 1634.

47 Late 13th-century tomb slab
Formerly recumbent, it is now set upright in the small enclosure on the south side of the choir. The use of incised lines for the decoration is typical of the period; the crosses on the later tomb slabs tended to be carved in low relief. The quatrefoil motif on this slab is paralleled in the south-wall window of the choir [**39**, **40**].

The cloister court and ambulatories

In its present incarnation, the cloister court at Bridgetown is surrounded on three sides – north, east and south – by buildings. The church is on the north side of the complex. This was its usual but not its exclusive position in this planning scheme; the church would have cast a shadow across part of the cloister had the arrangement been reversed. The cloister walks or passages would have been places of work as well as of reflection, with each passage having a particular range of functions. To take advantage of light from the south, desks and carrels for study and writing were placed along the wall of the church, and here part of the day was spent reading. The cloister walks also provided a setting for that most impressive of rituals, the Sunday procession.[136]

Bridgetown had no west range; rather, a high wall with a natural flood plain terrace behind it bounds the cloister. West ranges generally had store-rooms at ground-floor level, and here the provisions were kept under the management of the cellarer. On the first floor of west ranges in Benedictine and Augustinian houses there was accommodation for the head of the community and his guests, whereas in Cistercian houses the west range was given over to the lay brethren.[137] Bridgetown had no obvious provision for guests, and it is not inconceivable that among those earthworks on the river terrace,

48   View southwards along the vaulted cloister passage

49   The vaulted cloister passage viewed from the north-west

50 View northwards towards the
church along the vaulted cloister
passage

identified as possible remains of a nucleated settlement, are some which represent guest accommodation [20].

A vaulted passageway running along part of the east side of the cloister [48, 49, 50] was the principal means of access into the priory complex from the south side, although a well was later dug into the ground at the north end of the passage outside the entrance to the church [51]. The passageway has a pointed vault throughout. Two chamfered stones, one a jamb stone and the other an arch stone, survive *in situ* at the north end of the east wall of the passage, and clearly belong to a doorway across the passage which would have opened to the south into the passage itself. Although they have seen some conservation work, the quoins at the junction of the east wall of the vaulted passageway and that passageway which runs along the south end of the east range probably mark the former existence here of another doorway, probably also late medieval in date, sealing this end of the passage. A third doorway or a gateway may have sealed the vaulted passage immediately to the south of this. Its eastern respond survives, while its western respond would have been flush with the north wall of the refectory, and is represented today by an area of broken walling.

Three arched openings in the surviving stretch of this wall, each of them flanked by a sloping buttress, face into the centre of the cloister court, while one archway, located beside the refectory, opens onto what would have

51 The well outside the 13th-century
processional doorway into the
nave of the church
This feature was first exposed during
excavations by Dermot Twohig, and
was dug out to a depth of three metres.
An insubstantial wall crossing part of the
well was not recorded in the original
excavation record.

been the south walk of the cloister [**49**]. Each of the three openings has a segmental-pointed arch of undressed stone facing across the court, and a small vault of similar profile cutting into the vault of the passageway. Each opening has splayed sides and hammer-dressed quoins, but the angles and lengths of the splays are not consistent. The buttresses are clearly added to an original outer wall surface, and their sides, which are flush with the sides of the arched openings, are themselves splayed, but they do not continue the lines of the earlier splays, thus giving each opening an irregular double splay. The inconsistency in the length of what survives of each of the original splays suggests that the outer face of the passage had been damaged somewhat before the buttresses were added to it. The original outer wall surface, with two corbels still projecting westwards from it, is preserved above the arched openings, indicating that the original thickness of this wall was about 50cm, although it must be said that we cannot assume that this part of the wall was not refashioned when the buttresses were built.

The vault in the passageway is typically late medieval, and is likely to be contemporary with the walling along the east side of the passageway off which it springs. It is not clear, however, if it is contemporary with the west wall of the passage and with the arched openings in it. While one might argue that the west wall here predates the vault, and that when the vault was added the buttresses were built in order to support it, the interpretation favoured

52 The internal west wall of the cloister
This wall is riddled with rows of cavities, none of them original. The fabric of the wall suggests it has seen several repairs.

53   The south side of the church nave
The cavities in the west wall of the
cloister continue along this side of
the court.

here is that the vault is contemporary with the west wall and its arched openings, and that the buttresses were added sometime later, probably after the wall had fallen into disrepair.

Corbels and projecting stone courses along the north, west and south boundary walls of the cloister court indicate that the cloister walk in these areas was roofed with sloping wooden roofs [**52**, **53**], although, somewhat enigmatically, there are also corbels on the outer wall of the passage on the west side of the east range. More enigmatic still are some springing stones of a vault tucked into the north-west corner of the cloister, running for 130cm along the west end of the south wall of the church. Contrived as it may seem, we may be reduced to explaining it as an aborted late-medieval attempt to create a vaulted passage along the north side of the cloister. The remaining three sides of the cloister, which apparently had lean-to roofs, as was observed earlier, seem to have been arcaded, to judge by some of the *ex situ* stones preserved at the site and by the stone now preserved in the Protestant churchyard in nearby Castletownroche [**54**, **55**, **56**, **57**].

The cloister court at Bridgetown is located to the south of the church, and is flanked by domestic buildings on the east and south. Clearance in the late 1970s revealed a number of features in the area of the court, but they are now reburied. Recorded only on a plan of the priory made by Dermot Twohig at that time [see **27**], their stratigraphical relationships to each other and to

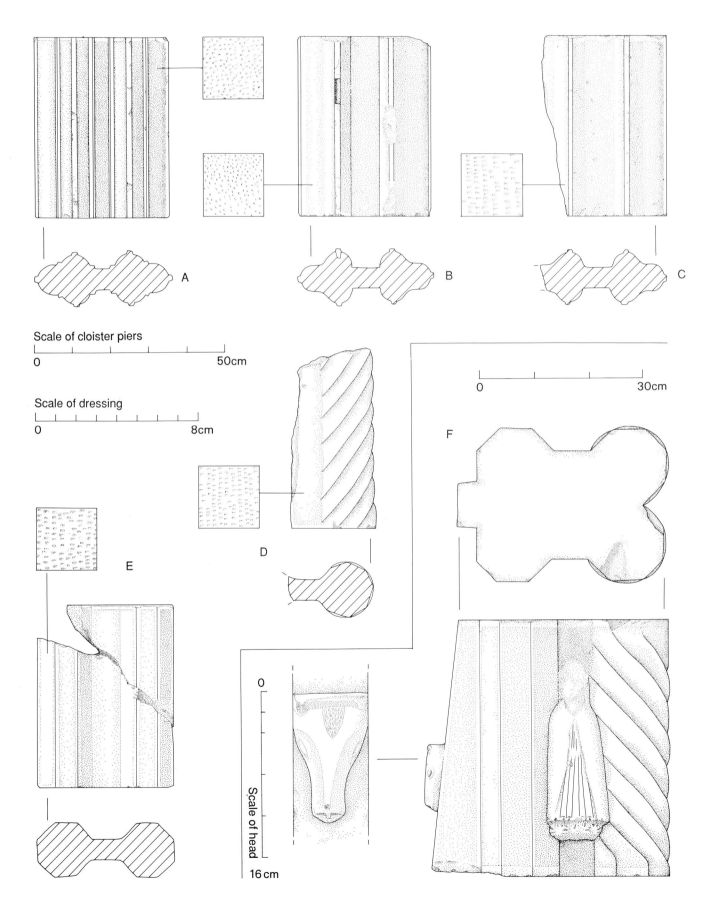

Scale of cloister piers

0   50cm

Scale of dressing

0   8cm

0   30cm

A

B

C

D

E

F

0

Scale of head

16 cm

No less than five variants on the classic dumb-bell pier survive from Bridgetown. Only one corner pier (the decorated example in the grounds of the Church of Ireland at Castletownroche) and one capital now remain from the arcade.

other features of the priory, including the destroyed cloister arcade (discussed below), are not known. The narrow concrete ledge, which today defines a trapezoidal area in the cloister court, was put in place after the clearance work of the late 1970s but seems not to relate to any of the features Twohig observed.[138] One of the features Twohig revealed, the well, has since been re-exposed [**51**].

Nine stones survive from a late-medieval cloister arcade for which there is no structural evidence on site today [**54**, **55**, **56**, **57**]. The piers are of the typical late-medieval 'dumb-bell' form.[139] A cloister stone was recorded in a photograph in March 1992, but disappeared from the site shortly afterwards, while another stone bearing carvings of a small robed figure and a stylised animal head is preserved in the Protestant churchyard at Castletownroche. The latter two stones, each of which is embellished with pairs of contiguous cylindrical and polygonal mouldings at their corners, are probably piers from the return angles of a cloister arcade; the cylindrical mouldings have spirals. Crofton Croker, who illustrated the stone which is now in Castletownroche, also illustrated other cloister fragments which are now lost. One of these may have been part of one of the corner piers; one of the two cylindrical mould-ings has a network of crossing lines rather than spiralling. The other fragment appears from his drawing to be a single column, and is decorated with hori-zontal bands of zig-zag ornament.[140]

G

55   56
57

55   Corner pier, Bridgetown Priory
     cloister arcade
     This pier was stolen from the site in
     March 1992. Its present location is
     unknown.

56   A capital from one of the cloister
     piers [see **54e**]

57   An unusual variant on the
     'dumb-bell' cloister pier,
     with twin rolls at the edges
     The plant scroll terminates in a small
     triskele.

The east range

The east range at Bridgetown was one long building of two storeys [**58**, **59**], set at an unusual angle relative to the other structures of the monastery. The upper storey was the dorter or canons' dormitory, located here for ease of access to the choir. Awoken by a bell, the brethren formed a procession, walked down a stairway into the church, proceeded to the choir stalls, and then celebrated Matins and Lauds. They returned to the dormitory and were again awoken, this time for Prime.

The principal access into the lower storey of the east range was through the doorways opening off the east side of the cloister. The northernmost of the three well-preserved doorways which open off the vaulted passage is 110cm wide and is chamfered externally (in other words, on the side of the passage), with a slight chamfer and rebate on the interior. The segmental-arched roof of the embrasure is preserved, but the original outer arch is lost and has been replaced with a modern rubble-built flat arch. There are clear indications that the jamb stones on both sides of the doorway are reused from other contexts; not only is the lowest jamb stone on the north not completely bonded into the wall, but it appears also to have two additional chamfers retained from an earlier usage, both of them partly hidden by the wall into which the jamb stone is set. Also, the lowest stone on the south side has a small bar-hole in it, which makes no sense in the context of a door jamb. The other two doorways, each 115cm wide, have pointed arches and chamfered surrounds. The central doorway of the three leads into the chapter house via a wide embrasure or lobby in the thickness of the wall, and is not central in that embrasure but to the south of it. The character of all three of these doorways indicates a late-medieval date, and these are such an integral feature of the walling in the passageway that the entire west wall of the passageway must be considered of the same date.

The lower stage of the east range was originally divided into several apartments of which the central one, distinguished by having the largest door and a cluster of three windows lighting it, was the chapter room [**60**, **61**]. So-named because it was here that a chapter of the Rule was read daily, the Chapter Room was the administrative nerve centre of the priory. A door, often flanked by a pair of windows, gave access here from the cloister walk (sometimes through a vestibule). All brethren gathered there every morning to hear a chapter of the Rule of the order read out to them, to discuss the day-to-day business of the monastery, and for confessions to be heard and punishments administered. Seating was provided around the walls, with a seat for the prior in the centre of the east side. Flanking the Chapter Room on both sides were at least two other apartments. The one to the north of the chapter house may have been a sacristy, where vessels and vestments for mass were kept, and the other, the parlour, was where talking was permitted, albeit for limited periods.

Separating the east range from the church at one end and from the south range at the other end were passages or slypes giving access to the cloister from the exterior east side of the complex. Somewhere along this range, a second flight of stairs, the day stairs, was used by the community when entering the dormitory from the cloister. Also in the east range was probably the novices' room, but which of the apartments served this function is no longer clear. The walls of the upper-storey dormitory are substantially rebuilt, and one cannot be certain the four windows in its east wall, including the twin-light above the chapter room [**61**], are authentic in form or position.

———

58   The east range,
       looking northwards

opposite

59
60   61

59   The east range,
       looking southwards

60   The exterior east wall of the
       east range
       The rebuilding of much of this wall,
       particularly the upper parts, is evident
       here.

61   The three later 13th-century
       chapter room windows with a
       dormitory window – rebuilt as a
       twin-light – above

The south range

The south range at Bridgetown is not confined to the southern side of the cloister but extends eastwards beyond the east range. The western part is comprised of a single two-storey building, containing at the upper-storey level the great dining hall or refectory [**62**, **146**]. The positioning of the refectory at upper-storey level, above an undercroft rather than at ground-floor level, as one might find in a Benedictine or Cistercian house, is typical of a house of canons regular, and might reflect the upper room in which Christ shared the Last Supper. The first substantial meal was dinner, eaten after Mass in late morning. Before entering the refectory, the brethren washed their hands at the lavatorium, a long basin supplied with running water. Usually the lavatorium was set into the wall of the refectory, as was the case at Bridgetown [**63**], but sometimes it was a free-standing structure set into the garth [**97**]. Silence was observed during meals, with one of the community reading aloud from holy writings from the pulpitum. Supper was eaten in the early evening after Vespers. The dais or high table in the Bridgetown refectory would have been at the east end, opposite the entrance and close to the pulpitum. The lower storey of this building – the refectory undercroft – was essentially a cellar.

The undercroft, which is the only part of the priory to have extensive (but corroded) remains of original medieval plaster, is divided by cross-walls into three chambers of regular size [**64**, **65**, **66**]. The entire undercroft appears to have been excavated by Twohig, but a photographic record survives only for the easternmost part [**66**] wherein the fragments of unfinished architectural sculpture executed in oolithic limestone were found [**12**, **29**]. Six arches ran lengthways along the centre of the undercroft, and these sprang from the end walls, from the cross-walls and from square piers centrally positioned in each of the chambers. None of these arches survives intact today. The arches and their supports are apparently insertions [**67**]. The end walls seem to have been mined away to contain the springers of the extreme easterly and westerly arches, suggesting that the arcade is an addition to the original building. The cross-walls seem to be contemporary with the piers and are not properly bonded into the side walls. Indeed, in order to facilitate the symmetrical placement of the piers and cross-walls it was necessary to partially block one of the windows – that contained within the pulpitum projection – though the execution of this was surprisingly inexpert. The insertion of these features into the building was certainly executed in the 13th century, and may even be contemporary with the erection of the east range. The span of the easternmost arch was reduced at a later stage in the building's history by the insertion of a narrower arch, facilitated by the addition of a projecting respond to the room's east wall and by an enlargement of the central pier. Contemporary with this change, perhaps, is the erection of a vault running east-west over the north-

62   The refectory building
      from the south-west
      The row of lancets lights the actual
      refectory; the lower windows and the
      doors, which have been inserted into
      window embrasures, serve the
      undercroft. The pulpitum projection,
      part of which collapsed in the late 1970s,
      is on the right of the building.

63   The entrance into the refectory
      building with the laver recess
      to the right
      The carved stone is missing from both
      arches, and the jambs of the doorway
      have been entirely rebuilt.

east space in the undercroft.

There are four different entrances into the undercroft, but the two in the south wall are definitely recent creations where originally there were windows; the fragmentary remains of the splays and segmental pointed arches can be seen. Of the other two entrances, the doorway in the west end of the north wall was the main entrance to the refectory. It has largely been rebuilt, but the original springer stones survive, apparently *in situ*, suggesting an original width of about 2.5m. The present, modern, segmental pointed arch appears to reflect the original arrangement. A second, smaller doorway at the east end of the refectory, leading into the passage, has lost its arch, but most of its chamfered jambs survive. The door here opened to the north, with the wall of the refectory cut back to receive it. One of the jamb stones on the north side is fashioned out of a 13th-century capital, possibly from the original

64 The western bay inside the refectory building viewed from the entrance doorway and showing an arcade pier in the undercroft

65 The central bay of the refectory building showing an arcade pier and inserted cross wall

east window of the church. This may be evidence that the doorway is a late-medieval insertion. The windows which provided lighting for this undercroft were, with one possible exception, tall, chamfered, rectangular openings set in segmental-arched embrasures. There are four windows of this type in the wall. The two windows converted into doorways were perhaps of the same type. The one window which seems to have been different is that to the east of the pulpit projection; there are fragmentary remains here of window seats on either side of the opening.

In the interior west wall of the building is a small segmental-arched doorway, 90cm wide, leading into a small lobby, and a stair turns to the right (or north) but is blocked after three (now broken) steps. This stair probably gave access to the upper storey of the refectory, but the point at which it opened into the upper storey is not clear due to substantial rebuilding of the

66 View of the interior of the refectory undercroft during Dermot Twohig's excavations
Twohig discovered pits and postholes beneath the undercroft floor [27]

67 Sections through the refectory building
Cross-section looking to the interior south wall (above)
Section through the interior showing the piers and cross-walls supporting the inserted arcade (below)

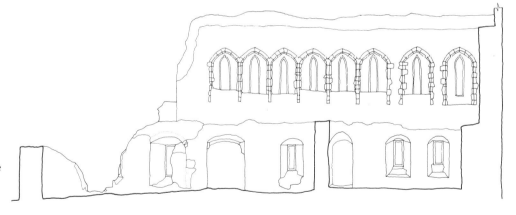

west and north walls of the refectory. The upper storey itself was marked by a setback in wall thickness on which the timber floor rested. Two windows appear to have provided lighting for this hall from the north side. Both are rebuilt with modern surrounds, and their exact date cannot be established. At least nine windows provided lighting through the south wall. One of these was in the pulpitum projection, but it was apparently blocked at some unknown stage of the priory's history. The remaining eight windows are along the wall to the west, and of these the two westernmost are spaced further apart than the remaining six. There were perhaps further windows to the east, but the walling here is destroyed. All these windows are pointed with external chamfers, rebates and relieving arches. The rear-arches of the six windows grouped close together share responds.

It is only in the south-east part of the priory complex that there is difficulty in identifying the functions of apartments. Kitchens normally flanked refectories, usually on the west rather on the east, but the square building which is immediately east of the Bridgetown refectory, and which is actually on the line of the east range, is tentatively identified here as having contained the kitchen; indeed, kitchens were normally square in plan.[141] The calefactory, or warming house – the only place in the priory other than the kitchen with a fire – was usually in this part of the complex, and in Bridgetown it may have been contained within the same square building as the kitchen, perhaps sharing its chimney flues. The rectangular building to the east at this end of the south range is rather more difficult to interpret. The presence of a drain running under its south-east end [**69**, **72**] suggests that here was the monastery's lavatory or rear-dorter, so-called because it was usually at the rear of the dorter, the canons' dormitory. In the late Middle Ages, however, the building seems to have accommodated the prior's private quarters at upper-storey level [**68**], and a tower was added [**24**]. The tower is three storeys high, with a wicker-built vault running east-west over the second storey. The north side of the lower storey of this tower was rebuilt in recent years as part of the conservation programme, so its original character is lost. It was doubtless entered from the north, but the nature of the access to the second storey is not now known. Inserted into the second storey is a round-arched doorway, now partially blocked, which opens southwards, presumably into the upper level of the small 16th or 17th-century building which is attached on this side. This is identical to the doorway leading onto the upper level of the tower at the northeast corner of the church. The upper storey in the prior's tower was reached by a spiral stair, its ascent beginning in the south-west corner of the second storey. This was clearly a high-status apartment; two fine rectangular windows cut in limestone with sharp external chamfers light it from the east and south, while the window facing west is a cusped ogee. Immediately west of the tower at upper-storey level in the rectangular building is a fine 15th-century window with cusps and an internal embrasure with seats. The window seat on the west has been partially rebuilt using other architectural fragments.

The south-east corner of this building at the south-east corner of the precinct has sheared away from the remainder of the structure [**68**], and tilts dramatically to the south and east. The tilt of this wall has been a feature of this corner of the priory for some centuries. A small 17th-century structure adjacent to the prior's tower was built against the leaning south wall after that lean had begun to form.[142] The style of the windows and the character of the masonry at this end of the building indicates late-medieval construction, but the fabric of the walls on the north and east sides is 13th century, and the second-storey window on the east wall is typical of that century. Indeed, archaeological investigations in 1992 revealed that original 13th-century fabric survives at lower-storey level inside a skin of late-medieval masonry.

68 The interior of the south-east building, looking south
This shows the remains of the private accommodation for the prior at upper-storey level.

Excavations of the south-east corner of the precinct

In 1992 a small archaeological excavation was carried out inside and outside the rectangular building at the south-east corner of the priory [**69**] with the hope of establishing the reason for the lean on the wall, and as a first step in exploring options for the building's consolidation. Two smaller cuttings, both 4m square, were made, one at the south-west end of the passage which leads into the west side of the cloister ambulatory from the exterior of the priory, and the other at the corner of the small 17th or 18th-century building which projects to the south immediately alongside the prior's tower. The former cutting established, as expected, that the passageway is an original feature of the 13th-century priory, while the latter established that the small building in question was erected upon a layer of cobbles, marked as layer D in **71**.

Cutting I was a long trench inside the building, kept narrow and comparatively shallow to prevent possible undermining of the adjacent walls. Cutting II was outside the building on its east side, and within it a smaller, deeper cutting was made (cutting IIa). Cutting II was a shallow excavation on account of its proximity to the river, which, during much of the duration of the excavation, was in flood. Cutting III was an L-shaped trench to the south of the building. The larger part of this ran east-west and was parallel to the leaning wall. This was machine-dug through silt and gravel riverine deposits to a depth of three metres, but on account of the tendency of the soil to sheer off vertically in large slabs, it was considered safest to backfill this quickly once it was apparent that the soil was sterile archaeologically. The other part of this cutting ran north-south and into the vaulted passageway which is in the thickness of the leaning wall.

69 Plan of the south-east building showing the location of the excavation trenches

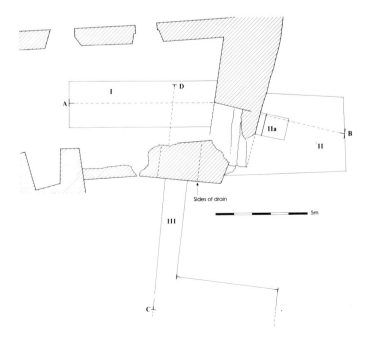

Cutting I

The stratigraphy encountered in this cutting is indicated in section A-B [70]. The strata which were identified and recorded beneath the present floor level were clearly post-medieval, and no original floor level was found. Two abandoned items of late-medieval stone-carving were found in the cutting, abutted by several strata, suggesting that the interior of the building had been used for dumping rubble. One was a limestone drip-stone identical to those which are preserved at the wall head on the north-side of the building and on the north side of the so-called prior's tower, and the other a 30cm-high limestone mortar with chamfered corners, originally free-standing [73]. Fragments of two small, 18th-century wine bottles were also found in a cache distributed through several contiguous strata at the eastern end wall of the building, and this, combined with evidence of small *in situ* fires amongst the rubble, suggests some very temporary occupation of the building's interior in the post-medieval period. Running north-south through the centre of the cutting was a low, highly compacted bank of rubble, probably the top of the vaulted drain. For reasons of safety this was not excavated.

Cutting II

This cutting, also illustrated in section A-B [70], was made outside the building; a smaller cutting, IIa, was made against the exterior east wall of the | building. The large cutting – excavated to a shallow depth as indicated above – yielded no archaeological material. Cutting IIa, however, revealed that the battered exterior face of the east wall of the building extended to a depth of 2.25m below modern ground level, and that much of this was originally visible; the 2m of soil excavated in cutting IIa is all post-medieval, and stratum L contains rubble from the medieval walls above. The batter itself, although pronounced in the manner of 13th-century base batters, is most likely to be late medieval in date. It conceals a wall-face which slopes inwards and is continuous with the 13th-century superstructure of the entire building.

Cutting III

There is also evidence of an original 13th-century wall-face having an outer skin applied to it in the 15th century in the south wall of the building [71]. For safety reasons it was not possible to excavate the entire fill of the vaulted drain [72] under the south wall, but enough of the fill was emptied to allow it to be entered and its construction examined. The outer arch and the passageway behind have segmental arches; most of the outer voussoirs are missing but otherwise the feature is well preserved. Examination of the interior revealed that the outer (or southern) 1.75m of the vaulted roof of the passageway had a mortared surface, while the inner part (or at least what could be

70   Section A-B
     (Note: The lowest level which the excavation reached is marked by a thick black line and annotated 'Edge of Cutting'. This line should not be interpreted as marking or indicating the shape of an actual archaeological boundary; it is simply the bottom of the cutting.)
a   Dark grey-brown (humic) layer
b   White mortar layer
c   Mid grey-brown layer
d   Black burnt layer
e   Orange-brown layer, very compact
f   Light brown gravel layer
g   Red-orange layer, very compact
h   Light-brown clay loam
i   Black-brown silty clay
j   Mid-brown gravel layer with mortar
k   Compact silty orange-brown, less stone inclusions than E above
l   Stone rubble
m   Orange-brown with iron staining

71   Section C-D
a   Natural boulder clay layer
b   Gravel and small pebbles
c   Layer of small stones
d   Layer of small cobbles
e   Silty orange-brown
f   Layer of small stones
g   Silty orange-brown, more small stones than E
h   Orange silt, stone-free
i   Thin, stony soil cover with rubble beneath

88

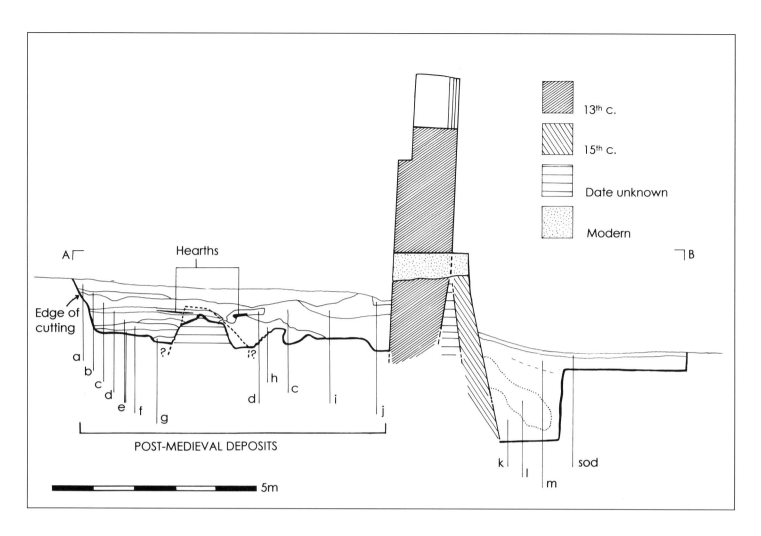

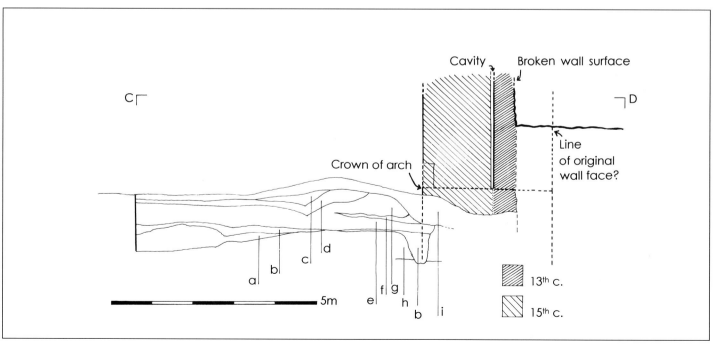

examined of it) had rubble voussoirs and seems never to have had a mortar coat. The junction of the two slightly different vaults marks the junction of the two walls, of which the innermost – and clearly the earlier – still has its wall-face intact, although hidden by the outer, later wall. It seems reasonable to date the earlier wall to the 13th century (contemporary with the upper-storey window in the east wall of the building) and the later wall to the 15th century (contemporary with the prior's tower). Particularly important is the evidence that the vaulted passageway, although 15th century on the outer face of the wall, is a feature of the original 13th-century building.

Immediately below the surface in cutting III was found a square sandstone block with typical 13th-century dressing, which was converted into part of a musket loop in the 17th century. Although its actual 17th-century context is not known, similar musket loops are a feature of all the buildings on the south side of the priory complex. Nonetheless, natural, undisturbed soil horizons were close to the surface in cutting III: layer H, a stone-free orange-coloured silt layer, had no obvious signs of having been affected by human activity, and appears to be stratified beneath boulder clay. If the vaulted passageway was a drain, as seems likely on comparative grounds, that drain clearly did not run off to the south. Is it possible that waste was allowed to accumulate outside the building at this point and that the builders simply intended liquid waste to seep away? There may even have been a pit to collect waste. Although concern for safety prevented a thorough excavation at this point, a small, stone-filled pit (B) was identified.

72 The exit of the vaulted drain during excavation in 1992

Ex situ stones

The 1992 excavations yielded comparatively few examples of worked stone, but clearance and partial excavation of the site under Dermot Twohig's supervision in the late 1970s explains the great quantity of *ex situ* stone now kept for safe keeping inside the tower at the west end of the church.[143] A number of these stones add considerably to our understanding of the priory, its building history and its architectural context, and are discussed below [**75**, **76**, **83**-**91**] and in other appropriate places in this work. Among the stones not illustrated and analysed here are many fragments of window sills, jambs and arches, externally chamfered and rebated in the 13th-century manner. Represented among these fragments may be up to six windows, the original positions of which cannot now be identified. Equally, two or three large, barred and glazed windows of late-medieval date are represented among the *ex situ* stones, and their former context is no longer known.

73 Pestles and mortars

Limestone mortar (A), dating from the late Middle Ages, found in the excavation of the interior of the building at the south-east corner of the priory; a sandstone mortar (B) and two sandstone pestles (C, D), all of unknown date, were among the *ex situ* stones at the site.

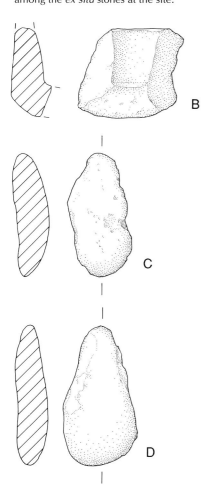

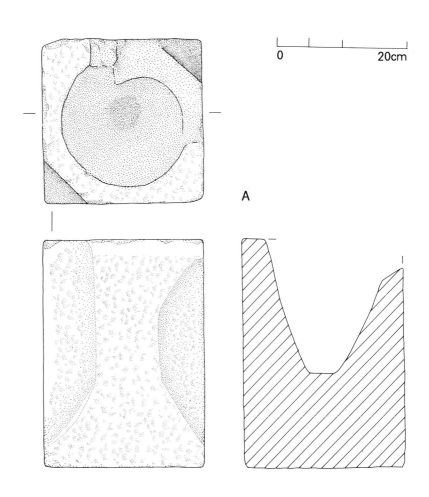

74 Piscina recess in the choir of
St Mary's, New Ross, Co Wexford
The fleur-de-lis decoration of one of the
capitals of this early 13th-century feature
is reminiscent of that on **75**.

75 Decorated basal stone
This stone, decorated with two registers
of fleur-de-lis ornament, has the same
shape as the bases of the mouldings
above the corbels of the east window
[**34**], but its provenance within the
original church is uncertain.

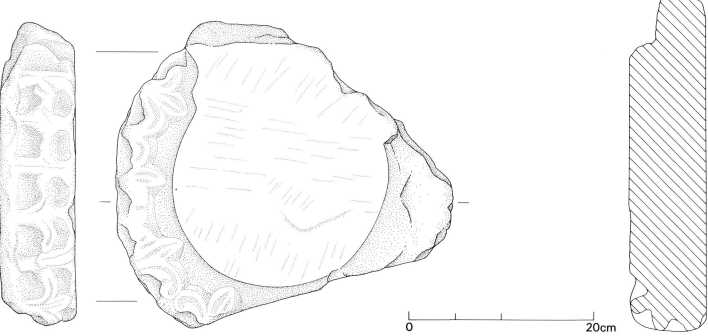

0   20cm

76 Decorated angle capitals

Each of these capitals, carved into the corner of a square stone, is decorated in typical Early English Gothic fashion, with small plant motifs springing from fillets. For an English parallel see **77**. Contemporary Irish craftsmen favoured zoomorphic motifs [**81**].

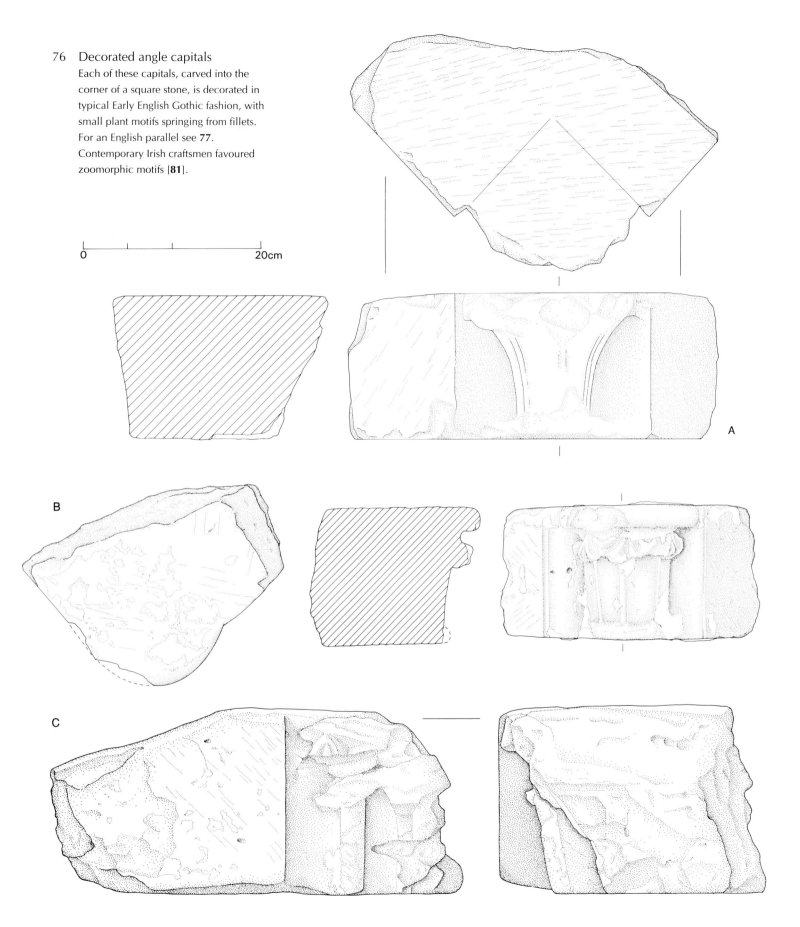

0   20cm

93

opposite

77 78
79 80

77 Early 13th-century capital from
    Sherborne Abbey, Dorset

78 Later 13th-century doorway at
    Athassel Priory, Co Tipperary
    Doorway into the vaulted parlour in the
    west range, showing spherical flowers
    used as stops on the hood moulding
    [see **79**, **80**].

79 Terminals of the internal hood
    moulding of a north-wall choir
    window
    The spherical flower used as one of the
    terminals (the other terminal is a more
    abstract version of this) is a typical
    decorative device of Early English Gothic
    in Ireland.

80 Terminals of the internal hood
    moulding of a window in the choir
    of St Mary's church, New Ross,
    Co Wexford

81 Early 13th-century capitals from
    Ballintober Abbey, Co Mayo
    An example of native Irish craftsmanship
    west of the Shannon at a time when the
    Anglo-Normans were settling in eastern
    Ireland, it shows the late-Romanesque
    penchant for zoomorphic motifs.
    Contemporary capitals in the early
    Gothic traditions used plant motifs.

82 Early 13th-century capitals from St
    David's Cathedral, Pembrokeshire
    Note how the fillets which are on the
    shafts below the capitals are continued
    onto the astragal (neckring) which
    separates the shafts from the capitals.
    The same feature is found on
    Bridgetown's finest capitals [**84**].

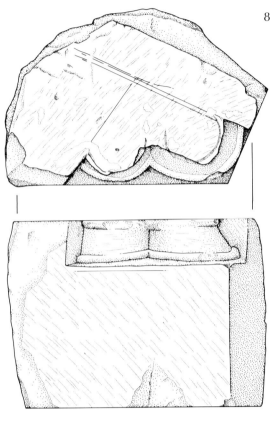

83 Twinned capital

This pair of capitals is set into the corner of a stone, the obtuse angle of which is equivalent to the splays on the original 13th-century east window. Lines scratched on the underside of the stone represent the stonemason's attempts to find the correct angle before carving the capitals; the angle of the stone is probably the reason for this trial and error [see also **84**]. He clearly had no difficulty marking out right angles [see **76a**]. The original placement of this within the priory is unknown. Almost identical to **83** is a block of stone with twinned capitals reset (inverted) at the top of one of the responds of the east window, and this may indicate the original provenance of both **83** and **84** (below), but the closely paired columns which would have descended from these capitals does not match with the moulding profile of the interior of the original window [**35**]. These capitals could possibly have come from the original exterior of the east window, in which case Bridgetown would probably have possessed one of the finest external east-end elevations of any medieval church in Ireland. The only part of the priory where windows of comparable quality to those in the east wall of the choir might be expected is in the chapter room, but these are rather too large and elaborate to have been used in a chapter house as modest as Bridgetown's.

0 ——————————— 30cm

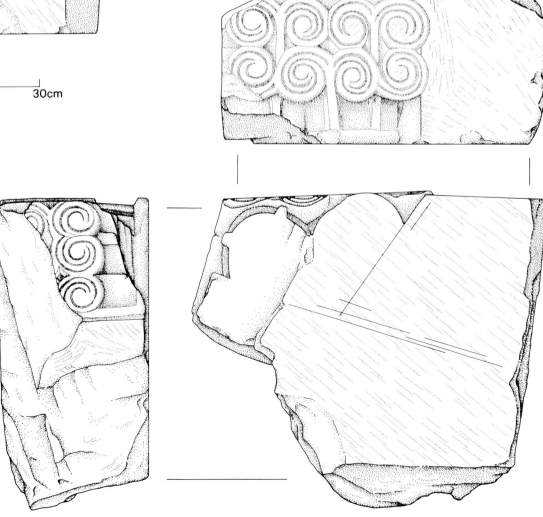

96

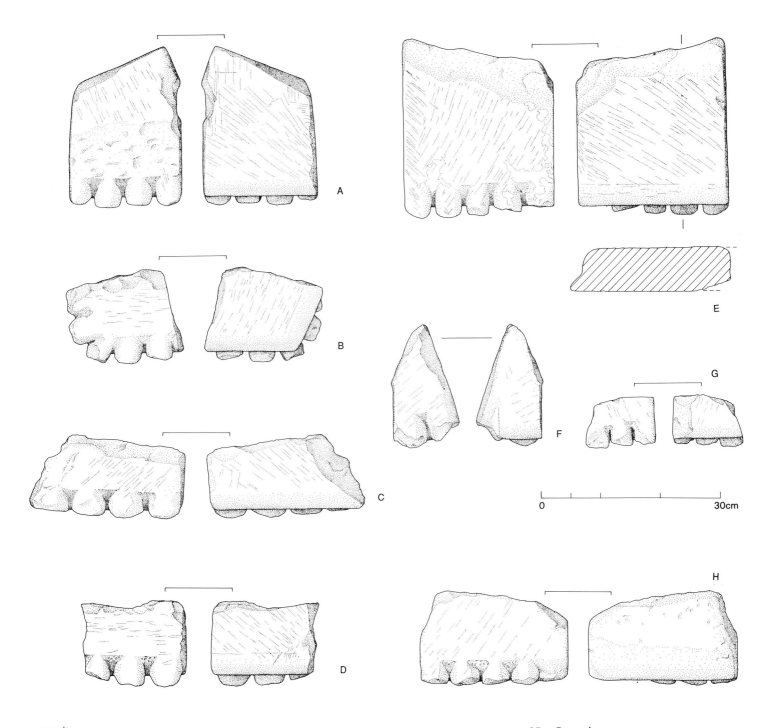

opposite

84 Decorated twinned capital

This stone, shaped to the same obtuse angle as **83** above, and presumably from the same context originally, has decoration which is unique: two parallel registers of spirals spring from fillets in the manner of plants [see **82**], but instead of being confined to the actual capitals, they colonise the flat face of the stone above the capitals. Could this extraordinary design have been concocted by an Irish mason working on the site?

85 Carved stones

These thin stones are decorated with an unusual billet motif (small semi-cylindrical bosses projecting at 90° from the edge of the stone). One of them (B) is cut at an angle, which suggests it comes from the same context as **83** and **84** above. Its thinness and its semi-convex profile suggests it was an abacus above a capital.

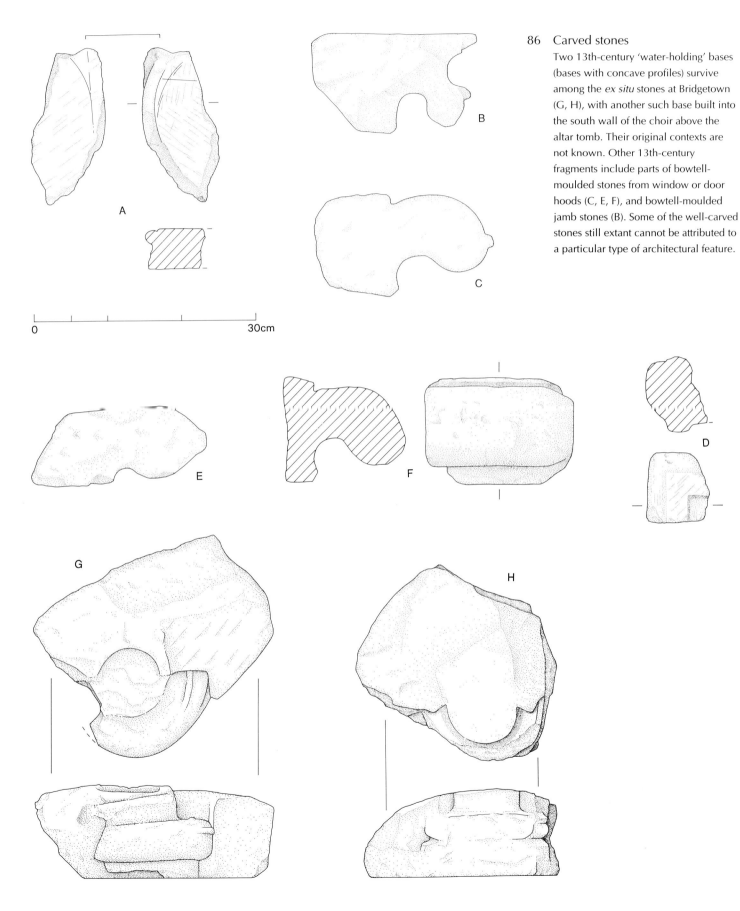

86 Carved stones

Two 13th-century 'water-holding' bases (bases with concave profiles) survive among the *ex situ* stones at Bridgetown (G, H), with another such base built into the south wall of the choir above the altar tomb. Their original contexts are not known. Other 13th-century fragments include parts of bowtell-moulded stones from window or door hoods (C, E, F), and bowtell-moulded jamb stones (B). Some of the well-carved stones still extant cannot be attributed to a particular type of architectural feature.

A

B

C

D

E

F

G

H

0   30cm

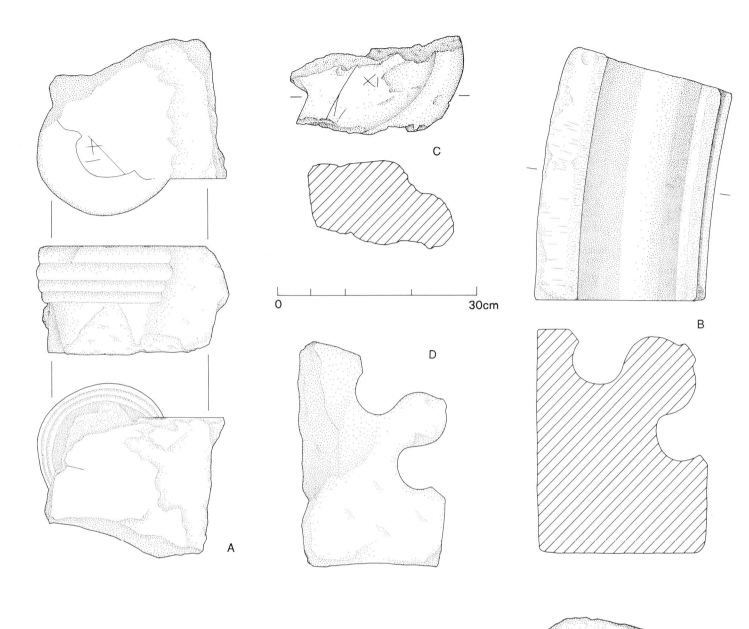

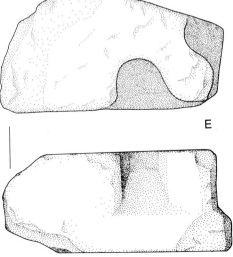

87 Carved stones

The carving on one of these stones (A) seems to represent a circular capital embellished with a series of four convex moulded rings. Instead of the corner of the stone being cut away to accommodate a descending column from this capital, that column descends as a projection from the angle of the stone. On the top surface of the capital, the mason has marked the outline of another architectural member, probably the springing stone of an arch and a small lining-up cross. The original context within the priory of this stone is unknown. The same mason may have carved an *ex situ* fragment from the base of the east window (C). Other stones from the original east window include bowtell-moulded voussoirs (B, D) and a bowtell-moulded jamb stone (E).

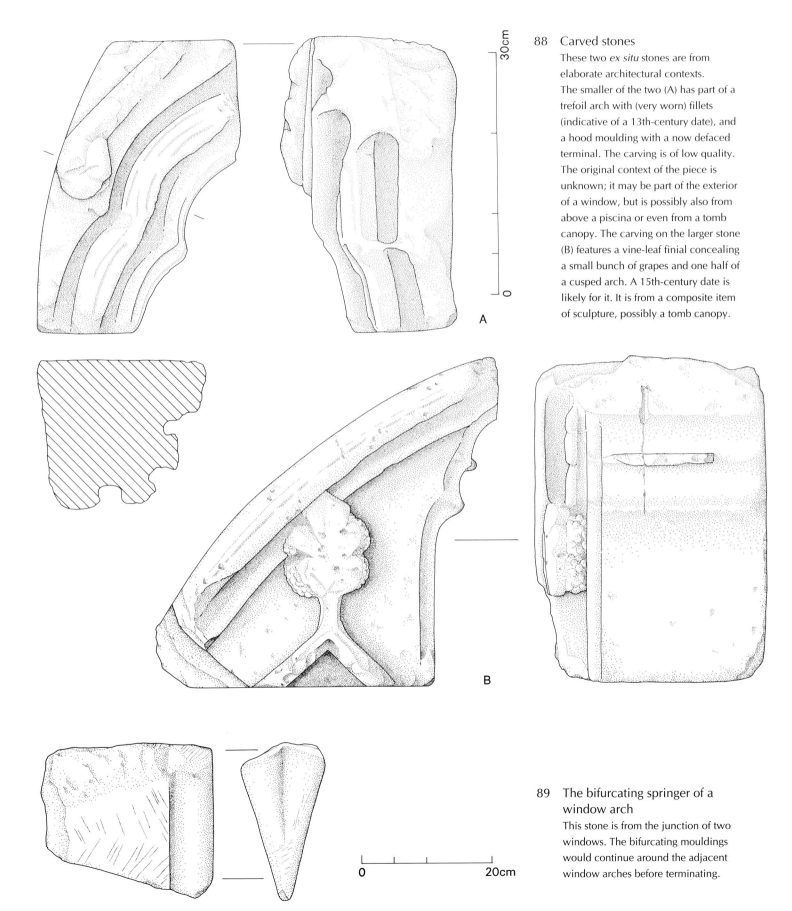

88 Carved stones

These two *ex situ* stones are from elaborate architectural contexts. The smaller of the two (A) has part of a trefoil arch with (very worn) fillets (indicative of a 13th-century date), and a hood moulding with a now defaced terminal. The carving is of low quality. The original context of the piece is unknown; it may be part of the exterior of a window, but is possibly also from above a piscina or even from a tomb canopy. The carving on the larger stone (B) features a vine-leaf finial concealing a small bunch of grapes and one half of a cusped arch. A 15th-century date is likely for it. It is from a composite item of sculpture, possibly a tomb canopy.

A

B

89 The bifurcating springer of a window arch

This stone is from the junction of two windows. The bifurcating mouldings would continue around the adjacent window arches before terminating.

0   20cm

90 Fragments of cusped windows

At least three cusped windows of late-medieval date survive among the *ex situ* stones. One of these fragments (C) was retrieved from recently rebuilt walling beneath the prior's tower, beside which a window of similar type is still *in situ*.

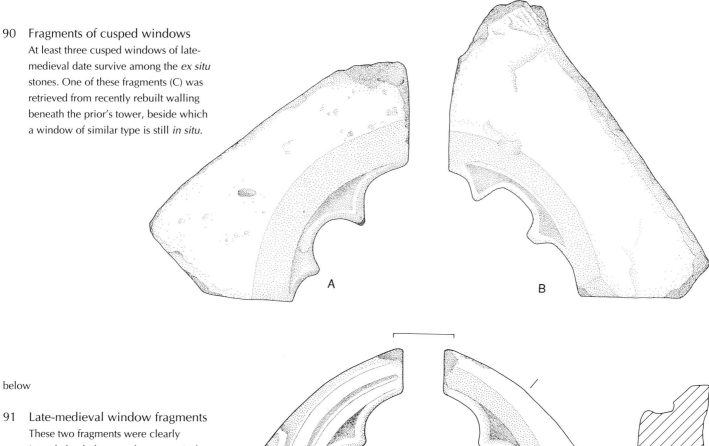

below

91 Late-medieval window fragments

These two fragments were clearly intended to belong on the same window, but the awkward curve of the arch on the larger fragment might suggest that this part at least was abandoned before it left the mason's workshop. The Lady chapel has two windows of similar vintage.

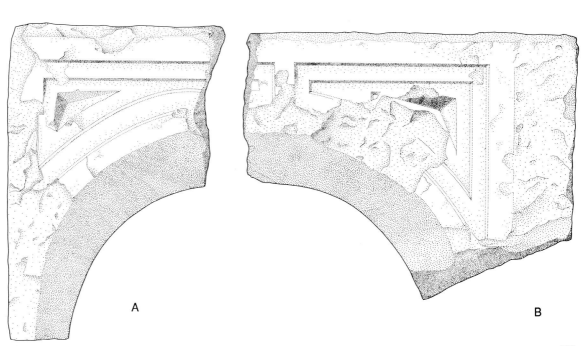

Building Bridgetown Priory

An itinerary around Bridgetown Priory reveals each of its elements to have quite a complex structural history. To begin the integration of these individual histories into a single story of the monastery's development, we might return to the circumstances of its foundation, the role of its patron, the identity of its builders, and the challenges posed by the site.

In not building a west range, the builders may have addressed the restrictions imposed upon the monastery's layout by the actual site it occupies. For the purposes of drainage, the monastery needed to be located on the flood plain rather than on a high river terrace, but the flood plain is quite narrow where the monastery is positioned, and in order to retain the essential character of the claustral plan, the idea of giving the monastery a range on its west side had to be jettisoned in favour of a high retaining wall against the terrace. If one range was dispensable in a claustral plan, it was the west range: none of the essential parts of the monastery was ever placed along that side of the cloister, and where there were *conversi* (lay brethren), as in a Cistercian monastery, they were housed in the west range. That eastward extension of the south range, which is such a strong feature of the site plan, may in turn have been in response to the lack of space on the west side of the monastery, but even this was not an adequate solution to the spatial problems inherent in the site. The river was still too close, and by the late Middle Ages some rebuilding was necessary in the south-east corner of the enclosure [**71**], and the walls at the south end of the east range may even have twisted slightly due

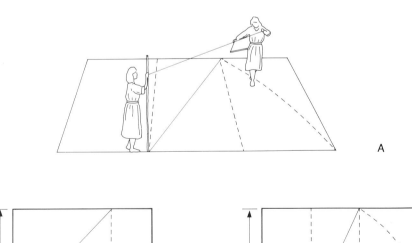

A

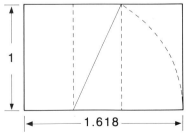

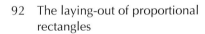

B   1.414

C   1.618

92 The laying-out of proportional rectangles
Medieval masons consistently laid out their structures according to two proportions, 1:1.414 and 1:1.618, both easily achieved by two men using ropes and pegs (A) to lay out a square and use its diagonal (B) or the diagonal of half the square (C) to create a rectangle.

to unstable foundations [**68**]. Even the presbytery extended too far to the east; although it seems to have suffered no structural problems arising out of its proximity to the river, the interior of the church can flood when the river is particularly swollen.

A patron like Alexander was doubtless involved with the monastic community in the process of deciding upon the form of the buildings, but responsibility for building the monastery lay squarely with the master mason or master of the works, normally a professional contractor. Clerics may well have helped in the building process. Little is known of master masons in medieval Ireland, and indeed the best-known person, Robert of Clairvaux, who built Mellifont, is exceptional in being a cleric; few of the English architects of the high Middle Ages were clerics.[144]

Fitting a monastery of claustral type into a restricted site was a challenge. A site needed to be able to accommodate a complex of buildings, with an overall square or rectangular ground plan. One might expect, *a priori*, that communities would also have been concerned that enough space was available to achieve a balance between the relative sizes of the different elements of the monastery, first in terms of their capacity to successfully contain the community, and secondly, in terms of their adherence to highly regulated mathematical schemata. However, there appears to have been little equilibrium between the size of the church choir, the refectory, the dormitory and the chapter room, although each of these structures was intended to accommodate the entire community at some stage of the monastic day.

The layout of Bridgetown in the 13th century

The first activity on the site of the priory may have been the construction of temporary wooden buildings, both for worship and for accommodation. Documentary sources do sometimes indicate that it was normal practice for the stone buildings to be preceded by wooden buildings, as is exceptionally well documented at the Cistercian abbey of Fountains in Yorkshire.[145] The only indication that the present buildings at Bridgetown were preceded by timber structures was revealed in Dermot Twohig's excavations inside the refectory. Here were found postholes, arranged in a manner which suggests that the timbers they held did not function within the present stone superstructure. The refectory may originally have had timber supports for its upper floor, but their postholes would be beneath the piers of the present undercroft arcade. The inadequacies of the excavation and the lack of a report on what was found make interpretation difficult, but assuming these postholes to belong to temporary accommodation on the site, the replacement of this building by the refectory would suggest that the mason had decided upon the size and layout

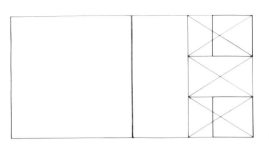

A

left

93 The layout of Bridgetown Priory: a reconstruction of the process

The entire priory complex can be contained within a grid of eight boxes, each with a proportion of 1:1.618. The north and south ranges occupy the north and south ends of these boxes, and each range is contained within a row of four boxes with proportions of 1:√2. The exact sequence of the laying out of the site is not known, but it is not inconceivable that the smaller boxes on the north side (the side of the church) were laid out first (A), and that the process was extended southwards across the site to create the grid (B, C). The priory buildings were fitted into the overall grid (D).

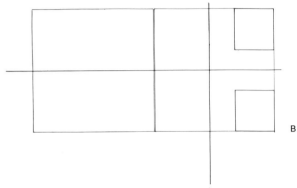

A

B

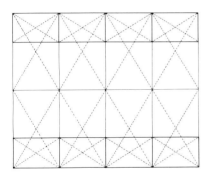

B

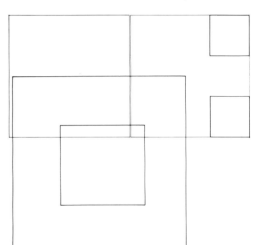

C

right

94 The layout of Athassel Priory: a reconstruction of the process

Analysis of the plan of Athassel reveals clearly that the church and cloister were laid out as two separate but integrated units. The church was laid out within two square boxes (A, B), that to the east being subdivided to facilitate the making of the presbytery and transepts. The position of the cloister was conditioned by the principal axes of the church (C); the larger square which defines the outer edge of the claustral range cuts across the middle of the two squares used to lay out the church, and on its eastern side it runs north-south through the middle of the square which used to arrange the east end of the church. The manner of this integration between the two parts of the priory complex (D) suggests that all the buildings were laid out about the same time, although the nave of the church and most of the claustral ranges were probably not built until after 1250.

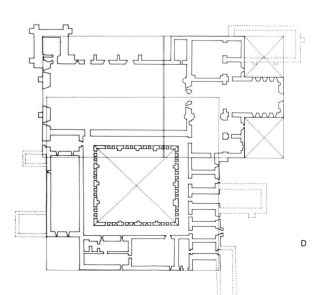

D

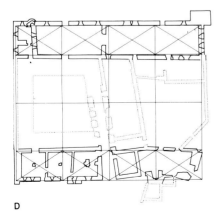

D

of the monastery before any stone buildings were erected.

The process of building in the Middle Ages was not based on ad hoc judgements of the relative proportions appropriate to the structures in question, but on tried and trusted proportional schemata of considerable antiquity, principal among them being those expressed by the ratios 1:1.4142 (or 1:√2) and 1:1.618 (the Golden Section).[146] These are mathematical expressions of long-used practical processes of laying out rectangles. Both involved the laying out of a square on the ground, marking the diagonal of the whole square or of half of it with a length of rope, then swinging the rope until it lined up with the side of the square [**92**]. Using the evidence of the standing buildings at Bridgetown, one can reconstruct the manner in which the plots of the buildings were prepared on the ground. Here the site appears to have had marked out on it two parallel rows of Golden Section 'boxes' separated by two contiguous rows of squares of related size [**93**], with the long church and the entire south range fitted into the former. The alignment of the refectory wall with the church's partition wall suggests that the east range was originally intended to run at right angles to the church and refectory, but in its present configuration, the east range can be assigned to a date later in the 13th century, and can be interpreted as a reconstruction of the original range involving the reuse of the original early 13th-century chapter house windows.

The system used for the layout of Bridgetown might usefully be contrasted with that which appears to have been used at Athassel. This larger and more complex monastery [**122**] was not laid out as a simple box subdivided into smaller squares and Golden Section 'boxes', as has been suggested for Bridgetown. Rather, the planning and construction began at the east end, and the cloister court was laid out using the same lines and proportions as had been used in the planning of the church's eastern limbs [**94**].

———

✠ 4

Augustinian Architectural Identities

Bridgetown Priory in context

THE EPONYMOUS INHERITORS OF BENEDICT'S RULE, THE BENEDICTINES, HAD little involvement with Ireland,[147] unlike in England where they specialised in constituting cathedral chapters. Among the few places where they were to be found was Cashel, Co Tipperary, where they may have served Cormac's Chapel, the royal chapel which Cormac Mac Carthaig had built between 1127 and 1134 [96].[148] Less than a century and a half later they were ejected from Cashel and replaced by Cistercians.[149] Benedictines may have remained a minority interest among Anglo-Norman landowners anxious to found monasteries in Ireland because Augustinians and Cistercians were already so well established.

It was the initiative of St Malachy of Armagh which brought Cistercianism into Ireland. He had visited Clairvaux and had forged a deep friendship with the order's leading light, St Bernard. Bernard's interest in Irish affairs is well attested in surviving documents, and his admiration for Malachy led him to write the Armagh man's biography, and even to advocate his canonisation. The Cistercians represented a colonial presence in Ireland – Bernard sent a Clairvaux monk, Robert, to oversee the foundation of Mellifont, Co Louth, in 1142 – and thus they prefigure the Anglo-Norman arrival of several decades later. Indeed, ethnic discord within the order, first manifest at Mellifont itself,[150] also signposts the troubles experienced by the Norman colony in the 14th century. What the Cistercians possessed, and what they carried with them to Ireland, was essentially a cultural package, of which a specific architectural style was but one element. Rigorous adherents to the monastic ideal, they brought their 'penchant for analysing a thing in order to discover its true nature'[151] to bear on architecture, producing large churches which, like their white habits made of undyed sheep wool,[152] were stripped down to what they regarded as the essentials, and they enacted legislation to ensure that it remained that way.[153]

Cistercian architecture was austere, bordering on severe, when viewed in comparison with the great cathedral churches or with the great Benedictine

and Cluniac churches of Continental Europe. But Mellifont may have been a new departure in architecture in Ireland in that no earlier use of the claustral plan is attested [**97**]. Its architecture (now largely reduced to foundations), like that of its successors, such as Jerpoint, Co Kilkenny [**98**], was considerably larger and technically more sophisticated than any stone building we know of prior to 1140. Intruded into a country which was slowly adjusting to the implications of a successful reform movement, Cistercian monasteries must have seemed quite revolutionary.[154]

The introduction into Ireland of the Rule of St Augustine – also through the initiative of Malachy – was without a colonial dimension. Native religious communities anxious to embrace the spirit of reform found the Rule to be inherently suited to adoption by clergy accustomed to other ways of living. There was no such thing as an Augustinian style of architecture before the introduction of the Rule into Ireland. St Augustine himself has long been a key figure among proponents of the iconographic approach to the interpretation of medieval architectural and its aesthetic. For those scholars who see the great churches of high medieval Christendom as expressions of spirituality, St Augustine's own writings lend themselves to architectural exegesis,[155] but they were not architectural manifestos. They did not generate particular architectural models. The variety of plans associated with the Augustinian canons in Ireland [**99**] is testimony to this.

previous pages

95 Kells Augustinian Priory from the south
The walled courtyard offered protection to the priory and its property in the 15th century. The enclosed area was known as the *villa prioris*, the prior's vill. It stands on higher ground than the actual church buildings; the claustral buildings occupy low ground in order to take advantage of the river, which is clearly visible behind the church.

96 The tympanum over the north portal of Cormac's Chapel, Cashel, carved *c*.1130
The Romanesque architecture of Cormac's Chapel owes much to the contemporary English tradition, a fact underlined by the Norman helmet of the centaur on the tympanum.

opposite

97 The lavabo at Mellifont
This Romanesque structure, located along the south edge of the cloister, served essentially the same function as the laver at Bridgetown [**63**]

98 The nave arcade at Jerpoint Abbey looking towards the crossing

99 Comparative plans of
    Augustinian monasteries[156]

A   Inchicronan, Co Clare
B   Ferns, Co Wexford
C   Kilmacduagh, Co Galway
D   Errew, Co Mayo
E   Killone, Co Clare (nunnery)
F   Inisfallen, Co Kerry
G   Inchcleraun, Lough Ree, Co Longford
H   Ballinskelligs, Co Kerry
I   Annaghdown, Co Galway
J   Killagh, Co Kerry
K   Cahir, Co Tipperary
L   Clareabbey, Co Clare
M   Newtown Trim, Co Meath
N   Molana, Co Waterford
O   Bridgetown, Co Cork
P   Athassel, Co Tipperary
Q   Clontuskert, Co Galway
R   Ballybeg, Co Cork
S   Canon Island, Co Clare
T   Monasternagalliaghduff,
        Co Limerick (nunnery)
U   Ballintober, Co Mayo
V   Kells, Co Kilkenny

In each case, the church is shown with
solid black walls.

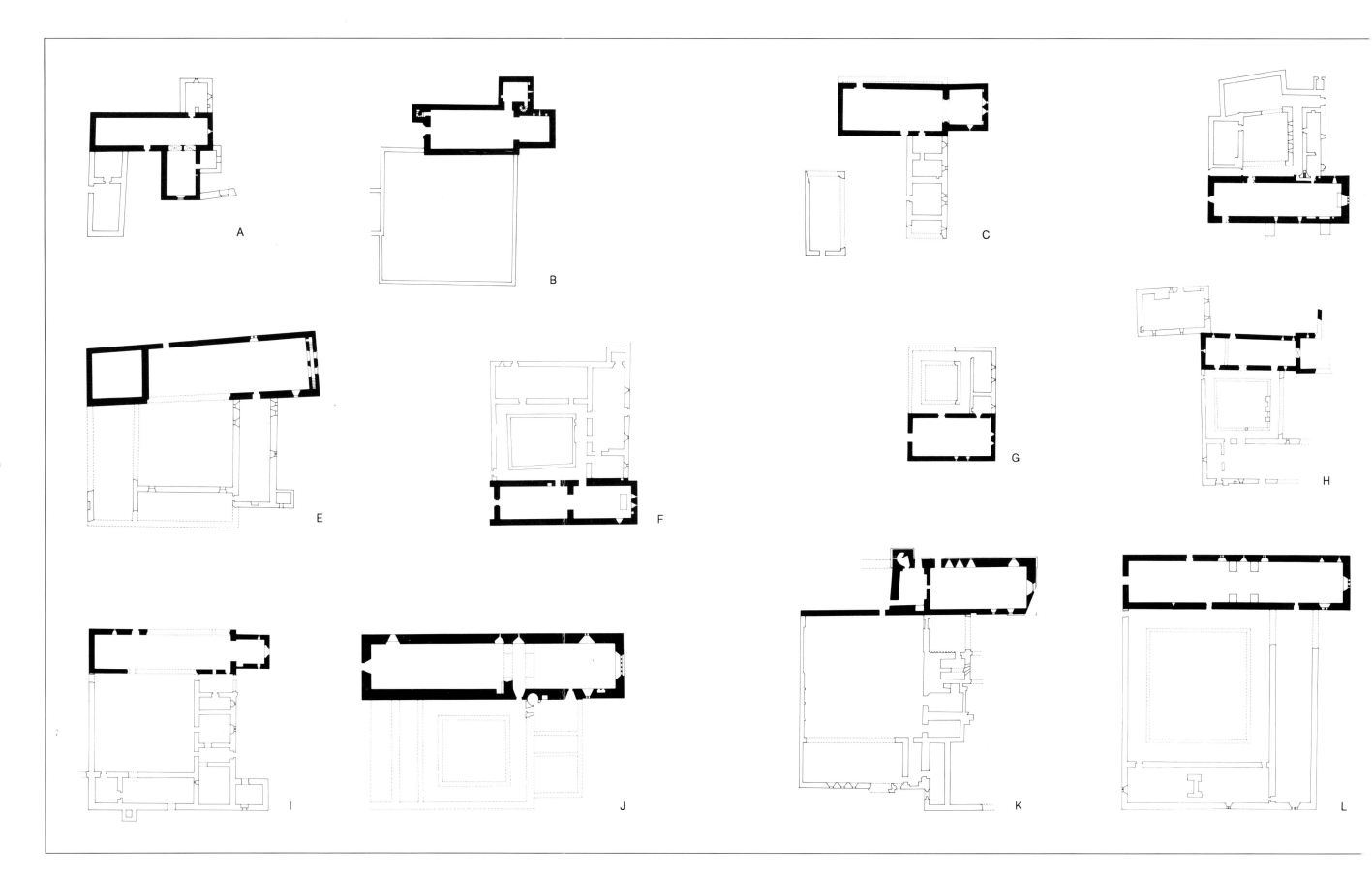

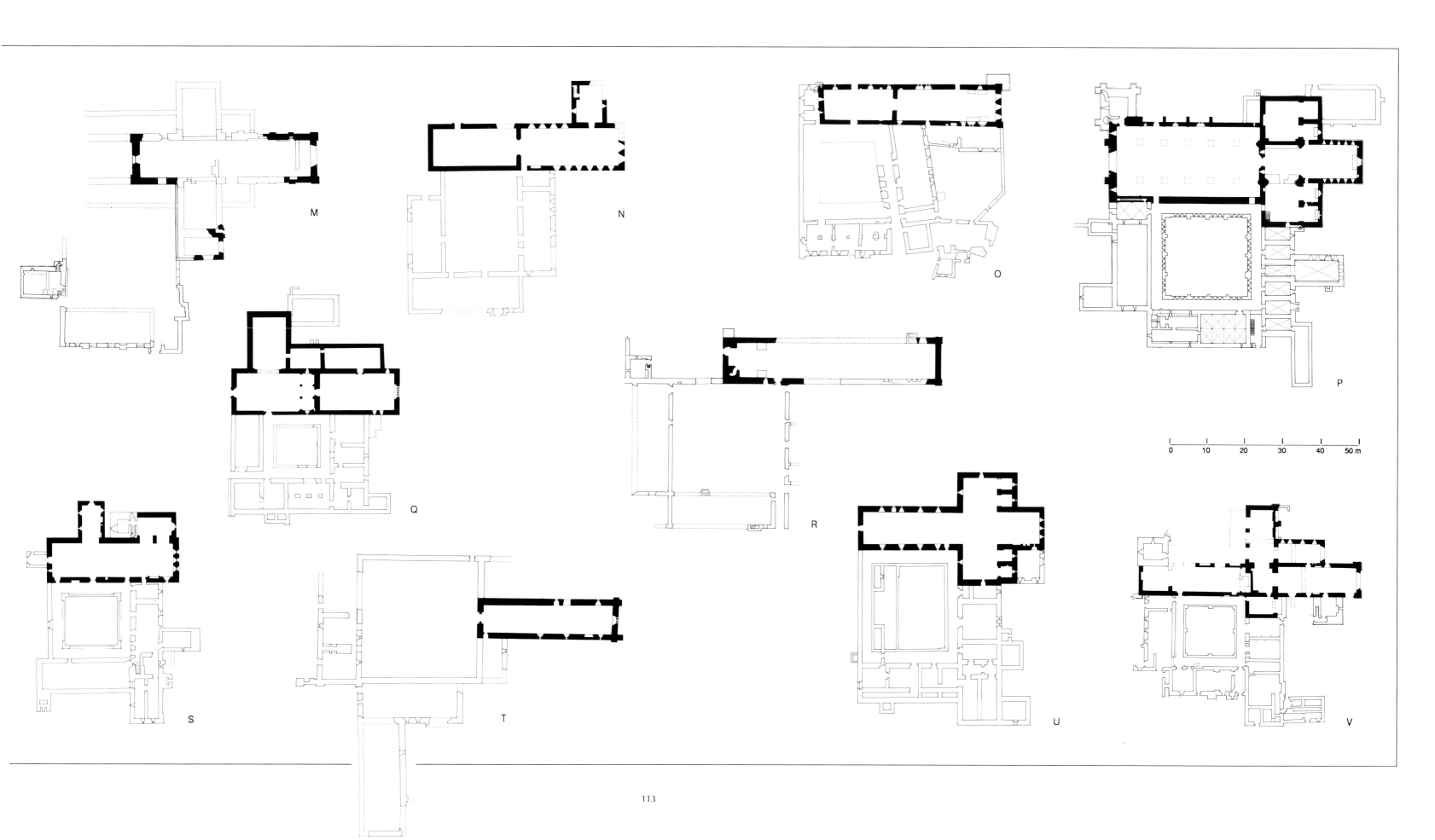

M

N

O

P

Q

R

S

T

U

V

The Romanesque style and the Rule of St Augustine

The reform of the native Irish Church did have an architectural manifestation prior to the arrival of reformed monasticism: the Romanesque style. The term Romanesque, which suggests a style of art and architecture connected fundamentally with the output of Roman artists in Antiquity, was coined to convey such an impression in the early 19th century by antiquarians who regarded it as 'degenerate Roman,' the final, debased manifestation of the Classical tradition.[157] The style emerged in Continental Europe in the context of the Gregorian reform of the mid-11th century. It entered Ireland in the early 12th century and was adopted by native craftsmen who combined its decorative forms and concepts with their own traditional, indigenous forms to create the hybrid known as Irish Romanesque [**100**].

The Irish Romanesque style was largely a southern phenomenon, and its birthplace, if not at Cashel [**96**], was at least within the Cashel archdiocese. The earliest churches in the style are at places in Munster which were chosen as diocesan centres by the reformers, or which claimed diocesan status having been overlooked by the reformers.[158] If, therefore, the emergence of a distinctive Irish version of the international Romanesque style of architecture and sculpture is so fundamentally linked to the creation of new dioceses, it is curious that no strong native Romanesque tradition developed within the archdiocese of Armagh, and that neither Armagh nor Bangor appear to have possessed Romanesque workshops of any significance. The native Irish Romanesque tradition never successfully colonised the archdiocese which had welcomed the Cistercians and the Rule of St Augustine. The reason was not a lack of communication between the senior clergy of the two archdioceses: Cellach, Malachy's predecessor as archbishop of Armagh, died and was buried in Munster, while Malachy himself served in the monastery at Lismore, Co Waterford, and enjoyed Cormac Mac Carthaig's patronage in the foundation of a new monastery in Munster, *monasterium Ibarense*.[159] Such contacts did, in fact, facilitate the spread of the Rule of St Augustine southwards; the monastery at Cong, Co Mayo, for example, adopted the Rule under Malachy's influence [**101**], and it then established a daughter house in Cork by 1135. The Irish Romanesque style was already in existence by the time the Rule reached the archdiocese of Cashel, and older monasteries in Munster which adopted the Rule built their new churches in the Romanesque style precisely because that was the current style.

The monastic way of life, properly followed, did mean adherence to a scheme in which the daily routine was optimised, and the sort of monastic life which the Rule of St Augustine offered fitted comfortably into the same claustral template as that used by the Cistercians. But to be an Augustinian one did not actually need to live within a claustral environment. The spread of the Rule of St Augustine across mid-12th-century Ireland was not accompanied by

100 **The Irish Romanesque façade of St Cronan's church, Roscrea**
The pedimented west door (with a statuesque figure, presumably of the patron saint, in the pediment), the pedimented blind arcading, and the chevron decoration are all devices imported from overseas Romanesque traditions, but the antae (projections of the side walls past the end walls) are inherited from the indigenous Irish architectural tradition.

101 **The east range of Cong Abbey viewed from the cloister**
The monastic buildings of Cong, rebuilt in the early 13th century, are deployed in a claustral layout, but the architectural details of the doorways and windows belong mainly within the native Irish Romanesque tradition, albeit in a late, western version of that tradition.

the spread of claustral planning. Indeed, there is no certain evidence that any Augustinian monasteries in Ireland were claustral prior to the Anglo-Norman arrival, and even in those parts of Gaelic Ireland which remained largely untouched by the Normans – at least before the second quarter of the 13th century – the claustral plan only appears after the colonists had actually arrived on the island [**101**].

The Gothic style: Anglo-Norman foundations of the late 12th and 13th centuries

The architectural style most closely associated with the Anglo-Normans in Ireland is the Gothic, although they continued to allow their sculptors execute Romanesque forms in some castles (such as Adare, Co Limerick and Nenagh, Co Tipperary, both *c.*1200)[160] and in a small number of churches established immediately after their arrival. The two styles, Romanesque and Gothic, can be seen side by side in the architecture and sculpture of the Cathedral of the Holy Trinity – Christ Church – in Dublin, the earliest cathedral architecture which we can attribute to the Normans.[161] Christ Church was originally founded when the see of Dublin was established by the Hiberno-Scandinavians in the early 1000s. Dublin became an archdiocese in 1152. Eleven years later, Lorcán Ua Tuathail, recently elected as the archbishop, chose Augustinian canons regular of the Arroasian observance to serve as his cathedral chapter. That Arroasians would engage themselves in episcopal duties here in Dublin and elsewhere in Ireland highlights the differences between the churches in England and Ireland: the Arroasians were not unlike the Cistercians in their desire for solitude, and only in Carlisle were Arroasians of England to be found serving as a cathedral chapter.

The great church itself was built with a grandeur repeated only rarely in medieval Ireland [**102**]. It is an aisled building of cruciform plan, with a six-bay nave, unaisled transepts, a two-bay choir, of which the eastern bay is rhomboid in plan, and a Lady chapel which projects eastwards of the choir and is flanked by two-bay chapels which continue the line of the side aisles [**103**]. Beneath the church is a crypt, with groin vaults supported by square piers.

The transepts and the western bay of the choir are original, later 12th-century works, executed in a very late version of the Romanesque style: both round and pointed arches are featured, and the sculptural embellishment is comprised of, among other forms and motifs, tubular chevron and historiated or stiff-leaf capitals. The architectural form is unmistakably English: the interior elevations are tripartite in arrangement, with passages tunnelling through the walls at triforium and clerestory levels [**106**], while the exterior corners of the transepts have the shallow pilasters which are *de rigueur* in larger English

102 **Christ Church Cathedral from the south**
The flying buttresses are not original but were built in the 1870s by George Edward Street, the cathedral's restorer, to support the nave vaults which he rebuilt.

103 **Christ Church Cathedral ground plan** [162]

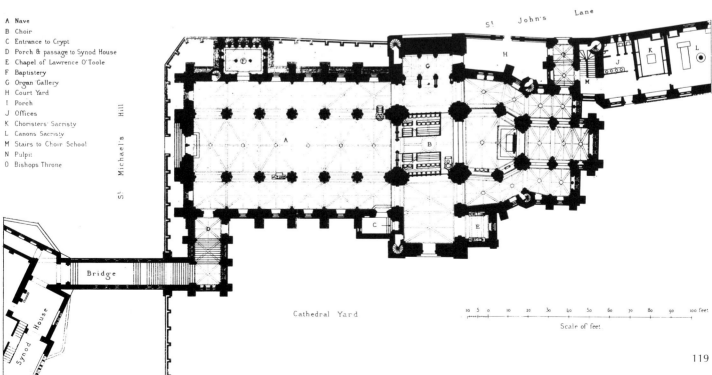

A Nave
B Choir
C Entrance to Crypt
D Porch & passage to Synod House
E Chapel of Lawrence O'Toole
F Baptistery
G Organ Gallery
H Court Yard
I Porch
J Offices
K Choristers' Sacristy
L Canons Sacristy
M Stairs to Choir School
N Pulpit
O Bishops Throne

St John's Lane

St Michael's Hill

Bridge

Synod House

Cathedral Yard

Scale of feet.

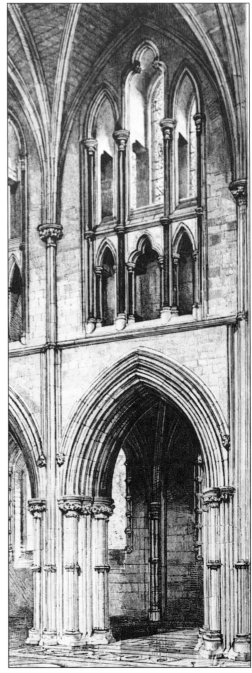

104 Interior view of the Gothic nave of
    Christ Church Cathedral, looking
    east[163]

105 A bay in the nave

opposite

106 The interior east wall of the
    Romanesque south transept of
    Christ Church Cathedral

Romanesque churches. Given that the Irish Romanesque style owes most to the stylistic tradition of early 12th-century England, it is strange that these features did not appear in Ireland until after the Norman arrival in Ireland. Of the pre-Norman churches of Ireland, only Cormac's Chapel reveals itself to have an ancestry in the same architectural tradition which produced Christ Church, but it does so only by imitating a triforium or clerestory in its use of stacks of blind arcading.[164] Winchester, St Alban's, Canterbury, Worcester and Bury St Edmund's, churches in which the eventual bishops in the late 11th or early 12th-century Hiberno-Scandinavian sees were trained, all had triforia, clerestories and wall passages, so it is appropriate that we should first see the format being used in Ireland in the cathedral church of a former Hiberno-Scandinavian see, but equally it is odd that it took the arrival of the Normans to make it happen.

Under Strongbow's patronage, the original Hiberno-Scandinavian church was allegedly given a new choir, a tower and side-chapels,[166] which suggests that the entire crypt and part of the superstructure of the east end

107 A plan of Christ Church Cathedral (crypt level) and a reconstruction of the adjacent claustral ranges[165]

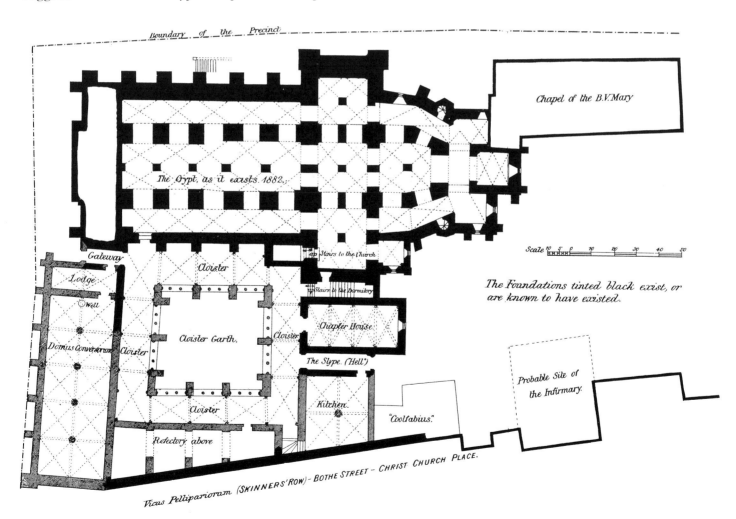

were built no later than the early 1170s. The earliest work we see today, however, is more likely to have been made during the archiepiscopate of bishop Laurence's replacement, John Cumin (1180-1212).

The nave, which is Early English Gothic [**104**, **105**], can also be assigned to Cumin. It had certainly been finished by 1234 when the church was allowed to be extended one bay to the west by the closing up of a street. Moreover, there is no crypt beneath the west bay of the nave [compare **103** and **107**]. The elements of the internal elevations of the nave have the same formal arrangement as those of the eastern limb of the church, but here the triforium and clerestory are integrated within triple-arched frames, one per bay, with each bay demarcated by a wall rib rising from ground level to the springing of the rib-vault [**105**]. This design has clear affinities in French Gothic architecture, but the retention of the mural passages, not only in the triforium but also tucked under the vault cells at clerestory level, is characteristically English. The source of the design is western England; indeed, the cathedral's entire sculptural repertoire – both Romanesque and Gothic – is western English in origin.[167]

A cloister with appropriate buildings was attached to the south side of Christ Church. This space was taken up with law court buildings in the early 17th century, and despite the claim that they contained quite an amount of medieval fabric, these were cleared away in preparation for the restoration of the cathedral.[168] Virtually nothing remains above ground now other than rebuilt foundations of what must have been a small but magnificent early 13th-century chapter house. These and other fragments, revealed in 1886, allow a comparatively small claustral precinct to be reconstructed on paper [**107**]. The cloister was certainly fairly narrow from east to west: it had to be tucked into the return of the transept at the east end, while its western ambulatory had to line up with the door at the west end of the south wall of the nave.

Christ Church's architecture was rivalled by that of Dublin's other medieval cathedral, St Patrick's, founded as a secular college by John Cumin, but with the probable intention (later realised under his successor, Henry of London) of achieving episcopal status.[169] The abbey of St Thomas the Martyr, located outside the city – as was St Patrick's – was probably as magnificent as either of the two cathedral churches. Like Christ Church, it was served by Augustinian canons, but their observance was Victorine, not Arroasian. St Thomas's began life in 1177 as a priory, being upgraded to abbey status about 1192. It was one of two places from which Bridgetown was settled. Unfortunately, nothing of it remains above ground, but one can be reasonably sure that its interior, at least the interior of its choir, was vaulted, and that its sculpture reflected a connection with England as faithfully and unambiguously as did Christ Church.

Much more survives of the contemporary cathedral church of Newtown Trim, also served by Victorine canons and also a parent of Bridgetown. Like

Christ Church, this was a cathedral priory, its bishop Simon de Rochfort having moved here from Clonard [108]. Like at Christ Church, its church was transeptal and may have been aisled in part, but its very long choir was not aisled. Lesser Augustinian foundations, such as Molana and Cahir [99], Ballyboggan [113] and Killagha [114], also had exceptionally long, unaisled choirs. The Newtown Trim choir had simple internal elevations: a string-course divides it into two horizontal registers or storeys, with the upper register divided into bays by thin shafts which opened out into vaulting ribs. These shafts did not extend to ground level [111]. Pilasters on the exterior walls and on the outer corners of the choir gave added strength to the vaults where the ribs might push back the walls. Despite the thickness of the walls, there was no mural passage. Without aisles, there was no particular need for clerestory lighting, and so lighting for the choir was provided by high lancets, one per bay, and each externally chamfered and rebated and set in wide splays with moulded surrounds.

West of the crossing at Newtown Trim, the upper walls were penetrated on each side by two mural passages, one above the other, corresponding to triforium and clerestory, and both lit. Vault ribs sprang from capitals attached to wall ribs with fillets [109, 110]. A string-course (also not found in the choir) ran at the level of the capitals, but the capital abaci do not continue the profiles of the string-course, as if inserted. The mural passages probably turned

108 Newtown Trim Cathedral and claustral ranges from the south

opposite

109 111
110 112

109 Wall shaft and springer for rib-vaulting, the lower mural passage, and parts of the clerestory windows in the south wall of the nave of Newtown Trim Cathedral

110 Wall shaft and springer for rib-vaulting in the south wall of the nave of Newtown Trim Cathedral

111 The choir of Newtown Trim Cathedral

112 The eastern part of the nave of Newtown Trim Cathedral showing the wall with which the nave was shortened in the late Middle Ages

113 Ballyboggan Augustinian Priory church, Co Meath

This extremely long church was constructed in the closing decade of the 12th century.

114 Killagha Augustinian Priory church, Co Kerry

The only substantial building to survive from an Anglo-Norman foundation of the early 13th century, the church had new windows inserted in the late Middle Ages.

into the transepts which are now gone, and they may well have crossed the large transept windows, as at Cashel Cathedral. A not dissimilar scheme is found in the east window of the choir at Killone, Co Clare [**115**].

Few Irish churches possessed the wealth of these three early Anglo-Norman foundations – St Thomas the Martyr, Newtown Trim and Christ Church. As works of architecture, at least two of these (and almost certainly all three) were exceptionally sophisticated, and while other churches – St Patrick's Cathedral in Dublin, or Duiske Cistercian Abbey in Graiguena-managh, Co Kilkenny – were of comparable artistic and technological quality, none surpassed them. The destruction of so much of the fabric at Newtown Trim and the lack of above-ground remains at St Thomas the Martyr leaves Athassel Priory, founded shortly after 1200, as the premier Augustinian ruin in Ireland.[170] In the early 13th century it must have rivalled the other two churches

115 The east window of the Augustinian nunnery of Killone, Co Clare

The round arches of this early 13th-century church demonstrate the late survival of the Romanesque style west of the Shannon.

116 Athassel Priory from the west
The bridge in the foreground is an original medieval structure.

117 The west façade of Athassel Priory church

in opulence, and the great walled courtyard in front of it, entered across a bridge and through a gateway [**116**], would have enhanced for a visitor the sense that this was a wealthy establishment.

The church dominates the complex, and was, by Irish standards, quite massive [**122**]. Its basic design is rather Cistercian in character: it is transeptal, with two chapels in each transept, and has a rectangular choir and presbytery, and an aisled nave originally of six bays. While much survives of the original fabric of the church, it is unfortunate that the nave and west façade, both constructions of the second half of the 13th century, have suffered considerable damage. The latter [**117**] was built to an accomplished design, with buttresses providing articulation as well as support, and a large central window providing abundant lighting above the original doorway. That doorway would have been similar to the fine 13th-century doorway leading into the crossing area further east within the church. Indeed, the latter shows signs of having been rebuilt, and it is not inconceivable that it is, in fact, the original west doorway of the church and that it was moved to the east end of the nave around the time the tower was built. The façade's symmetry was disturbed by the massive belfry on its west side, as happened also at Kells Priory [**128**]. A similar tower was built at the north-west corner of St Patrick's Cathedral, Dublin, in the 14th century. The façade of Llanthony Priory, Monmouthshire, although not exactly comparable, does give an impression of how imposing

118 The west façade of Llanthony Priory, Monmouthshire

119 The nave of Athassel Priory, looking westwards
Scars remain where wall shafts once supported vaults over the side aisles.

120 The crossing tower at Athassel Priory viewed from the west
(showing the doorway leading into the choir and the now-blocked rood above). The view from the nave of the high altar at the eastern end of the church [**125**] was restricted; the highly decorated doorway provided access to the choir through what was essentially a screen wall. Above this doorway was an open gallery, in the centre of which a crucifix once stood. This gallery was blocked when the upper part of the tower was added in the late Middle Ages to provide high-status private accommodation.

121 Athassel from the north-east

The destruction of the north half of the
crossing tower provides a good view of
the high vault inserted in the late Middle
Ages, and of the top of the south
crossing arch which had been blocked
to accommodate it. The north transept
and the Lady chapel, both largely
reduced to foundation level, can be seen
in the foreground.

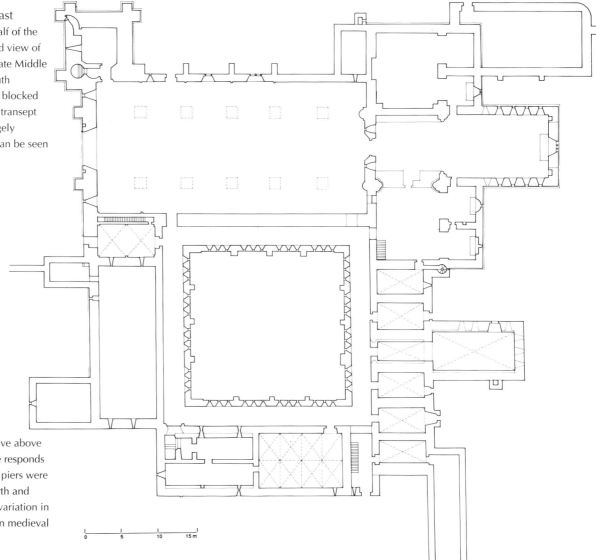

122 Plan of Athassel Priory,
Co Tipperary

The nave piers no longer survive above
ground, but it is clear from the responds
of the nave arcades that those piers were
not the same shape on the north and
south sides of the nave. Such variation in
pier shape is not uncommon in medieval
English parish churches.

0 5 10 15 m

123 The dormitory of Athassel Priory, looking south
The refectory is to the right, but is inaccessible directly from the dormitory. The apartment halfway along the dormitory to the left may safely be identified as that belonging to the prior.

124 The south transept of Athassel Priory showing the night stairs descending from the dormitory

opposite

125 The choir and presbytery of Athassel Priory
One of the great crossing piers is visible on the left; that on the opposite side is concealed in this view by a solid wall, intended to bear the weight of a vault inserted as part of the tower [**120, 121**].

the west wall of Athassel would have been [**118**]. The arcades of the nave were supported on piers of quatrefoil plan on the south side, and on piers of octagonal plan on the north side. The nave had rib-vaulted side aisles, as is apparent from the remains (and in some cases the scars) of wall shafts along the north side [**119**]. Curiously, these aisles did not lead directly into the transepts but terminated at the west walls of both north and south transepts. Whether the central vessel of the nave was vaulted is uncertain, but it is probable that it had a wooden roof from the outset. No scar remains of any roof, wooden or vaulted, on the west wall of the great crossing tower [**120**]. That tower was largely built in the 15th century to serve as domestic space, and the construction of a vault inside it necessitated the blocking of a unique rood gallery, but not of the 13th-century doorway leading towards the choir [**120**, **121**, **125**]. An unusual feature of the original crossing is the pair of screen walls separating the crossing from the transepts. The crossing arch on the south side is intact, but its supports – well-wrought, engaged half-quatrefoils – stand upon the crossing wall. Detailed study of Athassel's building history is required to make sense of this feature. Tall lancets provided abundant lighting for the early 13th-century presbytery and choir from both north and south, but the effect is somewhat diminished by the replacement of the original east window with a fairly simple three-light window. Unlike in many of the great English churches where later generations replaced the original east walls of churches with more up-to-date and more complex designs, here at Athassel, as at Bridgetown [**126**], a magnificent east window has had a modest successor. The niches at both ends of the east wall at Athassel appear originally to have served as aedicules for statues. The claustral buildings survive intact, including an extended chapter house above which was the prior's accommodation [**123**, **124**].

Kells Priory was almost as extensive as Athassel but was rather more

126 The east window at
     Bridgetown Priory

127 Kells Augustinian Priory
     from the south
     The walled courtyard offered protection
     to the priory and its property in the 15th
     century. The enclosed area was known
     as the *villa prioris*, the prior's vill.
     It stands on higher ground than the
     actual church buildings; the claustral
     buildings occupy low ground in order to
     take advantage of the river, which is
     clearly visible behind the church.

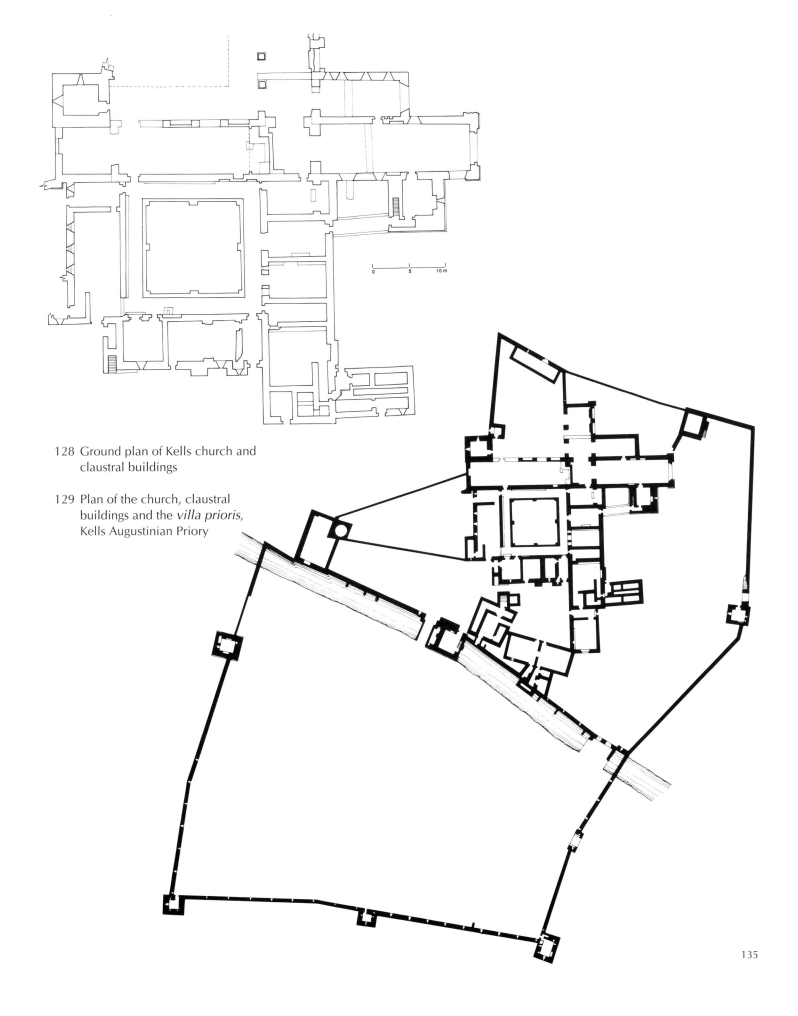

128 Ground plan of Kells church and claustral buildings

129 Plan of the church, claustral buildings and the *villa prioris*, Kells Augustinian Priory

130 A view of the crossing tower and north transept, Kells Augustinian Priory
By comparison with that at Athassel, the crossing tower at Kells is modest in scale and detail. There is no evidence that any part of the church was vaulted originally.

131 A view westwards from the choir, Kells

opposite

132 The church from the east, Kells
The high tower attached to the south side of the choir was evidently a prior's residence. Its construction necessitated the blocking of lancets lighting the choir.

modest. The great walled enclosure, almost perfectly preserved, dominates the site [**95**, **127**, **129**], but the church and the claustral buildings are ruinous, and this, combined with the fact that Kells appears to have had many alterations made to it over an extended period of time, makes analysis of its building history quite difficult [**128**].[171] As at Athassel, the church was transeptal. The north half of the church was quite spacious: an aisle existed on the north side of the nave, and it continued into the west side of the north transept [**130**]. The south transept was crammed between the square crossing – itself narrowed in the late Middle Ages [**131**] – and the east range. The long choir was lit by a fine row of lancets in the south wall and by a large window, now destroyed, in the east wall [**132**]. Whatever changes were made to the church in the course of the 13th and 14th centuries, the cloister seems not to have been upgraded from its original early 13th-century configuration, even as new structures were added to the south beyond the refectory. Unlike at Athassel, the chapter house remained as narrow as the apartments to either side of it.

Nearer to Bridgetown geographically and stylistically is Ballybeg Priory.[172] Unlike at Athassel and Kells, the church here was a long rectangle without aisles, and the choir and presbytery constituted about half its length. As at Newtown Trim [**112**], the church was shortened, leaving the plan of the priory rather imbalanced, with part of the cloister court left isolated to the west [**133**, **134**, **135**]. The cloister here was bounded by a vaulted passageway along its east side [**136**].

133 Ground plan of Ballybeg Priory

opposite

134 Ballybeg church, looking west
The west end of the church, with its fine 13th-century twin-light window, was later contained within a massive (14th century?) tower, left open to the east. A second, fully residential tower is visible further to the west through the twin-light window.

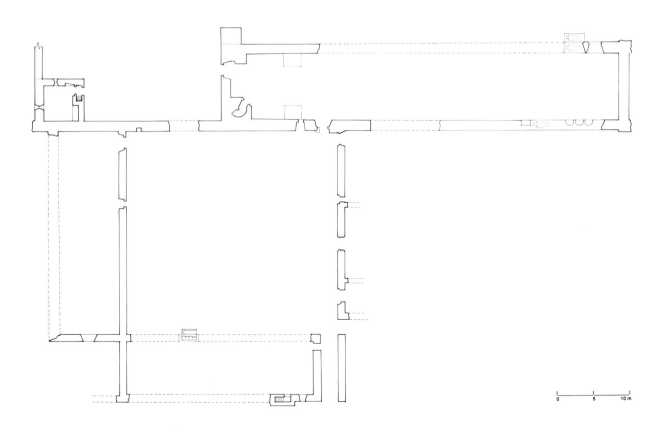

135 Ballybeg church viewed from inside the cloister court to the south

In its present form, the church does not extend any further west than the mid or late 13th-century twin-light window visible on the right, but it was originally longer. The entrance to the chapter house – a doorway of three orders of which only bases survive – is marked by a gap in the wall on the right. The fragmentary remains of the east end of the church are visible behind.

136 Ballybeg processional door, looking south

This doorway is located immediately east of the tower which now terminates the church. It originally opened onto the eastern cloister ambulatory, and that ambulatory was vaulted over (visible in the background), at least in part, as at Bridgetown [50].

137 The tower at the north-east corner of the church at Bridgetown

138 The belfry tower at Inistioge Augustinian Priory, Co Kilkenny
The chamfering at the top of the tower is unusual.

Some late medieval alterations

Ballybeg provides an illustration of one of two principal structural alterations made to these monastic houses in the Middle Ages: the insertion of towers. Ballybeg had two towers added, one along the length of the church, which effectively shortened it, and the other to the west at what would have been the original west end of the church [**134**]. The latter may well have been be the residence a prior, built after his church had been shortened. At Kells, a prior's tower is located not at a distance from the main liturgical activity at the east end of the church, but right against it and overlooking it [**132**]. In addition to the prior's tower at the south end of its precinct, Bridgetown had a tower inserted into the west end of its church, and another added to the north-east corner of the choir [**137**]. The positions of the towers varied. Athassel had, from the time the nave was constructed, a belfry tower beside the west façade [**117**]; a tower in the same position at Kells may be of the same date [**128**]. At Athassel, a tower seems to have been inserted over the crossing some time between the completion of the nave (in the late 1200s perhaps) and the later 15th century. Another belfry tower of massive construction was built at Inistioge Augustinian Priory [**138**] on the north side of the church.[173] At Clareabbey [**139**], dating from the 15th century, a central tower is reminiscent

139 Clareabbey, Co Clare,
viewed from the north

Almost entirely rebuilt in the 13th and
15th centuries, the original abbey of
Clare was founded by Domnall Mór
Ua Briain, a prolific founder of churches
and monasteries in late 12th-century
Limerick and Clare.

140 Cahir Priory, Co Tipperary,
viewed from the south-east

This late 12th-century Anglo-Norman
monastery was re-edified in the late
Middle Ages. Original early 13th-century
fabric survives in the church.

141 The fenestrated cloister at Athassel
Priory, looking westwards along
the south ambulatory

142 The east side of the fenestrated cloister at Errew Priory, Co Mayo

143 The reconstructed cloister arcade at Ballintober Abbey, Co Mayo

144 Cloister fragments – piers and capitals – at Buttevant Friary, Co Cork

of those used in contemporary Franciscan friary architecture in the western half of Ireland. Unlike at Clareabbey, where the crossing tower rises from within the walls of the church, the walls of the tower at Cahir [**140**] are flush with the church walls.

The second structural alteration made to many monasteries in the late Middle Ages was in the cloister itself. At Bridgetown, the east walkway of the cloister was vaulted in the late Middle Ages [**48**]. The nature of the openings in this covered walkway is rather difficult to establish, but the splays in the extant passage wall suggest that there was fenestration – as in the manner of Athassel [**141**] or Errew, Co Mayo [**142**] – along here, even though in their present form the openings are tall enough to walk through into the court. The other cloister walkways at Bridgetown were originally defined by a wall with elaborate arcaded openings. The extant fragments of characteristic dumb-bell piers [**54**] indicate clearly that in the late Middle Ages the Bridgetown cloister wall was arcaded in the manner of that at Ballintober [**143**], Buttevant [**144**] and many other monasteries of all orders.[174]

145 Exterior view of the vaulted passageway on the east side of the cloister at Bridgetown Priory

✠ 5

Mission Abandoned

The afterlife of Bridgetown Priory

B Y THE TIME OF ITS EVENTUAL DISSOLUTION IN 1541, BRIDGETOWN WAS A MOD-
estly valuable property. The jurors found that the priory, like many of
the other religious houses being assessed for confiscation at the same
time, was comprised of 'a church with belfry, dormitory, hall, buttery,
kitchen, cloister, and cellar, wit divers other chambers', all in ruins but 'necessary for the farmer'. Together with the cemetery, the priory covered two acres,
and was valued at 6s 8d without repairs. Also attached to the priory was 120
acres of demesne land, worth only 20s because the area was underpopulated,
with a water-mill worth 40s. The last prior, William Walshe, and others, held
six hundred acres of agricultural land in the townland, and there was, in addition, more than forty acres of woodland, but the population was low and
much of the land was waste, and the value of the land was much reduced as a
consequence. Three rectories attached to the priory were also deemed of little
value. The jurors set the value of the entire property at £12 16s 8d.[175]

After the monastery of Bridgetown was dissolved, a soldier, Robert
Browne, was leased the land, a grange and seven rectories to hold for twenty-
one years from 1545 at a rent of 40s. Browne was directed by the King to
'assign such portion of land to William Walshe, the late prior, as the [Lord]
Deputy and Council shall think requisite'. Walsh was given an annual pension
of less than £7 pending his promotion to a benefice of greater value than the
pension.[176] In 1565 Donal Mór McCarthy, newly created Earl of Clancarr,
requested of the earl of Leinster that he be given, along with either an annual
fee from the exchequer or some portion of land in the English Pale, 'as is customary for newly created earls', the priory of Bridgetown for the purpose of
being patron to spiritual promotions within what he described as 'my owne
countye of Clancarre'.[177] The priory and the rectories attached to it were granted in 1567 to William Bassenet and Richard Hunt to hold for twenty-one years
at an annual rent of £10 16s 8d.[178] In 1577 they sub-let the priory to Roger
Pope of Grangegorman, who then surrendered it to Sir Henry Sidney, the Lord
Deputy.[179] Elizabeth I then granted the lease of the priory and its possessions

to Sir David Lord Roche to hold for thirty years at a rent of £12 16s 8d.[180] Roche died in 1585, leaving £200 rent unpaid for the abbeys of Bridgetown,[181] Fermoy (Cistercian) and Glanworth (Dominican). His son, Maurice Lord Roche, was not charged with the arrears in recognition of the loyalty of his late father, and also of Maurice's own brothers who had recently died in the rebellions. Grattan-Flood suggested that, despite the accession of Browne and others to the property, the canons remained at Bridgetown until David Roche's death in 1585, if not Maurice Roche's death in 1600.[182] In 1595 Bridgetown was granted to Ludovick Briskett to hold for fifty years.[183] He was the last of the medieval owners or lessees of the property. Bishop Lyons of Cloyne, in his royal survey of 1614, reported that the priory, its 'church and chancel down', was in possession of Lord Roche and Sir Daniel O'Brien.

Grattan-Flood's assiduous researches bring the story beyond this point and into the modern era. He remarked that it was intended to build a Protestant church on the ruins about 1846, but that the project fell through. However, Grove White records the memory of such a church at Bridgetown, erected around the middle of the century close to the west side of the priory, adding that it was unroofed not long after being erected. More recent research indicates that this church was taken apart and its stones brought by cart to Ballyhooly, where, in 1880-81, they were reused in the small Protestant church there.[184]

The priory seems to have been in quite a state of disrepair during the 18th and, particularly, the 19th centuries. Crofton Croker visited the place in the early part of the last century. He made no remark on its condition, but he did trace the cloister and refectory without difficulty, adding that the former was 'now a naked square court used as a ball alley by the neighbouring peasantry'. Windele, who visited about the mid-1830s, wrote that the ruins were 'low, covered with ivy, and afford no picture'. He did not find the old priory uninhabited, however; an old woman and her two cats had, for the previous two years, been living in a tomb vault, and her food was supplied to her by the pitying local people.

Less than a century later, the Very Rev Michael Canon Higgins, parish priest of Castletownroche from 1901 to 1911, was lamenting the state of the ruins. The ruins were, at that stage, the property of the Church Temporalities' Commissioners, but Higgins complained that they gave no protection to the ruins and that the place was ivy-covered and falling down. The attention paid to the priory since the late 1970s, and especially in the 1990s, has reversed the long trend of neglect.

———

previous pages

146 The refectory building at Bridgetown Priory viewed from the south-west
The row of lancets lights the actual refectory; the lower windows and the doors, which have been inserted into window embrasures, serve the undercroft.

pages 150-151

147 Bridgetown Priory from the north

Selected Bibliography

RSAI Jn.   *Journal of the Royal Society of Antiquaries of Ireland*
IHS   *Irish Historical Studies*
Cork Hist. Soc. Jn. *Journal of the Cork Historical and Archaeological Society*
UJA   *Ulster Journal of Archaeology*
IER   *Irish Ecclesiastical Record*
RIA Proc.   *Proceedings of the Royal Irish Academy*

* indicates a publication relating specifically to Bridgetown

———

Clapham, AW, 'Some minor Irish cathedrals', *Archaeol. Jn.* (*Supplement Memorial Volume to Sir Alfred Clapham*, 1949).

Cochrane, R, 'Notes on the Augustinian Priory of Athassal, County Tipperary', *RSAI Jn.,* 39 (1909) 279-89.

Coppack, G, *Abbey and Priories* (London 1990).

Dickinson, JC, *The Origins of the Austin Canons and their Introduction into England* (London 1950).

Empey, CA, 'The sacred and the secular: the Augustinian priory of Kells in Ossory, 1193-1541', *IHS,* 24, 94 (1984) 131-51.

Greene, J, *Medieval Monasteries* (Leicester 1992).

* Grattan-Flood, WH, 'Augustinian Priory of Bridgetown, Co Cork', *Cork Hist. Soc. Jn.,* 22 (1916) 120-6.

* Grove White, J, 'Bridgetown Parish (Ballindrohid or Villa Pontis)', *Cork Hist. Soc. Jn.,* 15 (1909) 305-16.

Gwynn, A, and Hadcock, ND, *Medieval Religious Houses: Ireland* (Dublin 1970).

* Higgins, M, 'Bridgetown Priory, County Cork', *RSAI Jn.,* 35 (1905) 73-4.

Jeffries, H, 'The founding of Anglo-Norman Cork, 1177-1185', *Cork Hist. Soc. Jn.,* 91 (1986) 26-48.

Lawrence, CH, *Medieval Monasticism* (London 1984).

Leask, HG, *Irish Churches and Monastic Buildings II: Gothic Architecture to AD 1400* (Dundalk 1960).

Leask, HG, *Irish Churches and Monastic Buildings III: Medieval Gothic – The Last Phases* (Dundalk 1965).

Lynch, JH, *The Medieval Church: a brief history* (London & New York 1992).

* MacCarthy, CJF, 'Norman Times: Bridgetown Priory of the canons of St Victor I', *Mallow Field Club Jn.,* 12 (1994) 134-52; 13 (1995) 132-6.

* MacCarthy, CJF, 'In Norman Times: Bridgetown Priory of the canons of St Victor II', *Mallow Field Club Jn.,* 13 (1995) 132-6.

McCotter, P, 'The sub-infeudation and descent of the Fitzstephen/Carew moity of Desmond I', *Cork Hist. Soc. Jn.,* 101 (1996) 64-80.

McCotter, P, 'The sub-infeudation and descent of the Fitzstephen/Carew moity of Desmond II', *Cork Hist. Soc. Jn.,* 102 (1997) 89-133.

* O'Connell Redmond, G, 'Alexander Fitz Hugh: Founder of the Augustinian Priory of Bridgetown, Co Cork', *Cork Hist. Soc. Jn.,* 22 (1916) 168-71.

* Power, C, 'Bridgetown Abbey', *Mallow Field Club Jn.,* 6 (1988) 48-55.

Robinson, DM, *The Geography of Augustinian Settlement in Medieval England and Wales*, 2 vols (Oxford 1980).

Stalley, RA, *Architecture and Sculpture in Ireland 1150-1350* (Dublin 1971).

Stalley, RA, 'Irish Gothic and English Fashion' in J Lydon (ed.), *The English in Medieval Ireland* (Dublin 1984) 65-86.

Tietzsch-Tyler, D, *The Augustinian Priory of Kells, Co Kilkenny: An Exploration* (Freshford 1993).

List of Illustrations

1   Stone head carved in oolithic limestone
2   Bridgetown Priory from the south-west
3   Location map of Bridgetown Priory
4   Plan of Bridgetown Priory drawn by Revd M Horgan
5   Bridgetown Priory from the south
6   Drawing of Hugh of St Victor
7   Doorty Cross, Kilfenora, Co Clare
8   St Mary's Priory, Louth
9   Annaghdown, Co Galway
10 17th-century image of a Victorine canon
11 New Augustinian houses in Ireland, 1169-1320
12 Alexander fitz Hugh?
13 Aerial view of Bridgetown Priory from the north
14 The medieval county of Cork and the cantred of Fermoy
15 The base of a baptismal font
16 The choir of Molana Priory church
17 The partition wall between the nave and choir
18 The choir of Buttevant Friary church from the south-east
19 Bridgetown Priory location map
20 Earthworks at Bridgetown Priory
21 Newtown Trim, looking eastwards along the river Boyne
22 Bridgetown Priory from the north-west
23 The Refectory viewed from the east
24 The Prior's Tower
25 Aerial view of Bridgetown Priory from the south
26 Reconstruction drawing of Bridgetown Priory as it may have appeared in the late Middle Ages
27 Ground plan of Bridgetown Priory showing the principal functions of different parts of the complex
28 Principal phases of construction at Bridgetown Priory
29 *Ex situ* sculpture from Bridgetown Priory
30 Bridgetown Priory from the north
31 Interior of the nave, looking eastwards to the partition wall
32 Interior east wall of the choir
33 Exterior east wall of the choir
34 A corbel with a plant terminal on the east window at Bridgetown Priory
35 Plan of the east window
36 The east window of St Mary's parish church, New Ross, Co Wexford
37 Windows at Tintern Abbey, Monmouthshire, in the Decorated style
38 Panels from the façade at Tintern Abbey, Monmouthshire, in the Decorated style
39 Window at Bridgetown Priory in the Decorated style

40 The Roche tomb and twin-light window in the south wall of the choir
41 Late 15th or early 16th-century grave slab in the choir showing an unusual pattern of tracery
42 Part of the late 15th or early 16th-century grave slab built into the Roche tomb
43 Late 15th or early 16th-century grave slab in the choir
44 The Roche tomb, adjacent door and 13th-century window as they appeared in the early 20th century
45 The Lady chapel, looking eastwards
46 Late 13th-century tomb slab
47 Late 13th-century tomb slab in the small enclosure on the south side of the choir
48 View southwards along the vaulted cloister passage
49 The vaulted cloister passage viewed from the north-west
50 View northwards towards the church along the vaulted cloister passage
51 The well outside the 13th-century processional doorway into the nave of the church
52 Internal west wall of the cloister
53 The south side of the church nave
54 Cloister arcade fragments
55 Corner pier, Bridgetown Priory cloister arcade
56 A capital from one of the cloister piers
57 An unusual variant on the 'dumb-bell' cloister pier, with twin rolls at the edges.
58 The east range, looking northwards
59 The east range, looking southwards
60 The exterior east wall of the east range
61 Three later 13th-century chapter house windows with a dormitory window – rebuilt as a twin-light – above
62 The refectory building from the south-west
63 The entrance into the refectory building with the laver recess to the right
64 The western bay inside the refectory building showing an arcade pier in the undercroft
65 The central bay of the refectory building showing an arcade pier and inserted cross wall
66 View of the interior of the refectory undercroft during Dermot Twohig's excavations
67 Sections through the refectory building
68 The interior of the south-east building, looking south
69 Plan of the south-east building showing the location of the excavation trenches
70 Excavations – section A-B

71	Excavations – section C-D
72	The exit of the vaulted drain during excavation in 1992
73	*Ex situ* stones – pestles and mortars
74	Piscina recess in the choir of St Mary's church, New Ross, Co Wexford
75	Decorated basal stone
76	Decorated angle capitals
77	Early 13th-century capital from Sherborne Abbey, Dorset
78	Later 13th-century doorway at Athassel Priory, Co Tipperary
79	Terminals of the internal hood moulding of a north-wall choir window
80	Terminals of the internal hood moulding of a window in the choir of St Mary's church, New Ross, Co Wexford
81	Early 13th-century capitals from Ballintober Abbey, Co Mayo
82	Early 13th-century capitals from St David's Cathedral, Pembrokeshire
83	Twinned capital
84	Decorated twinned capital
85	Carved stones
86	Carved stones
87	Carved stones
88	Carved stones
88	Bifurcating springer of a window arch
90	Fragments of cusped windows
91	Late-medieval window fragments
92	The laying-out of proportional rectangles
93	The layout of Bridgetown Priory: a reconstruction of the process
94	The layout of Athassel Priory: a reconstruction of the process
95	Kells Augustinian Priory from the south
96	The tympanum over the north portal of Cormac's Chapel, Cashel, carved *c.*1130
97	The Lavabo at Mellifont
98	The nave arcade at Jerpoint Abbey, looking towards the crossing
99	Comparative plans of Augustinian monasteries
100	The Irish Romanesque façade of St Cronan's church, Roscrea
101	The east range of Cong Abbey viewed from the cloister
102	Christ Church Cathedral from the south
103	Christ Church Cathedral ground-plan
104	Interior view of the Gothic nave of Christ Church Cathedral
105	A bay in the nave, Christ Church Cathedral
106	The interior east wall of the Romanesque south transept of Christ Church Cathedral
107	A plan of Christ Church Cathedral (crypt level) and a reconstruction of the adjacent claustral ranges
108	Newtown Trim Cathedral and claustral ranges
109	Wall shaft and springer for rib-vaulting, the lower mural passage, and parts of the clerestory windows in the south wall of the nave of Newtown Trim Cathedral
110	Wall shaft and springer for rib-vaulting in the south wall of the nave of Newtown Trim Cathedral
111	The choir of Newtown Trim Cathedral
112	The eastern part of the nave of Newtown Trim Cathedral
113	Ballyboggan Augustinian Priory church, Co Meath
114	Killagha Augustinian Priory church, Co Kerry
115	The east window of the nunnery of Killone, Co Clare
116	Athassel Priory from the west
117	The west façade of Athassel Priory church
118	The west façade of Llanthony Priory, Monmouthshire
119	The nave of Athassel Priory, looking westwards
120	The crossing tower at Athassel Priory viewed from the west, showing the doorway leading into the choir and the now-blocked rood above
121	Athassel from the north-east
122	Plan of Athassel Priory, Co Tipperary
123	The dormitory of Athassel Priory, looking south
124	The south transept of Athassel Priory showing the night stairs descending from the dormitory
125	The choir and presbytery of Athassel Priory
126	The east window at Bridgetown Priory
127	Kells Augustinian Priory from the south
128	Ground plan of Kells church
129	Plan of the church, claustral buildings and the *villa prioris*, Kells Augustinian Priory
130	View of the crossing tower and north transept, Kells Augustinian Priory
131	Vew westwards from the choir, Kells
132	The church from the east, Kells
133	Ground plan of Ballybeg Priory
134	Ballybeg church, looking west
135	Ballybeg church viewed from inside the cloister court
136	Ballybeg processional door, looking south
137	The tower at the north-east corner of the church at Bridgetown
138	The belfry tower at Inistioge Augustinian Priory, Co Kilkenny
139	Clareabbey, Co Clare, viewed from the north
140	Cahir Priory, Co Tipperary, viewed from the south-east
141	The fenestrated cloister at Athassel Priory looking westwards along the south ambulatory
142	The east side of the fenestrated cloister at Errew Priory cell, Co Mayo
143	The reconstructed cloister arcade at Ballintober Abbey, Co Mayo
144	Cloister fragments at Buttevant Friary, Co Cork
145	Exterior view of the vaulted passageway on the east side of the cloister at Bridgetown Priory
146	The refectory building at Bridgetown Priory viewed from the south-west
147	Bridgetown Priory from the north

Notes and References

1   D Doggett, 'The medieval monasteries of the Augustinian canons regular' in *Archaeology Ireland*, 10, 2 (1996) 31; CA Empey, 'The sacred and the secular: the Augustinian priory of Kells in Ossory, 1193-1541' in *IHS,* 24, 94 (1984) 131. For Franciscan and Cistercian architecture respectively, see C Mooney, 'Franciscan architecture in pre-Reformation Ireland' in *RSAI Jn.*, 55 (1955) 133-73; 56 (1956) 125-69; 57 (1957) 1-38, 103-24; and RA Stalley, *The Cistercian Monasteries of Ireland* (London & New Haven 1987).

2   A model of this approach is JP Greene, *Norton Priory: The Archaeology of a Medieval Religious House* (Cambridge 1989).

3   M Higgins, 'Bridgetown Priory, County Cork', *RSAI Jn.*, 35 (1905) 73-4; J Grove White, 'Bridgetown Parish (Ballindrohid or Villa Pontis)', *Cork Hist. Soc. Jn.,* 15 (1909) 305-16; WH Grattan-Flood, 'The Augustinian Priory of Bridgetown, Co Cork', *Cork Hist. Soc. Jn.,* 22 (1916) 120-6; O'Connell Redmond, 'G Alexander Fitz Hugh: Founder of the Augustinian priory of Bridgetown', *Cork Hist. Soc. Jn.,* 22 (1916) 168-71; C Power, 'Bridgetown Abbey', *Mallow Field Club Jn.,* 6 (1988) 48-55; CJF MacCarthy, 'Norman Times: Bridgetown Priory of the canons of St Victor, *Mallow Field Club Jn.,* 12 (1994) 134-52; 13 (1995) 132-6.

4   Published first by Grove White, 'Bridgetown Parish'.

5   Acts of the Apostles (2, 44-5).

6   The practise and diffusion of monasticism in the late Antique and early medieval worlds is discussed in W Braunfels, *Monasteries of Western Europe* (London 1972) 13-36, and CH Lawrence, *Medieval Monasticism* (London 1984) 1-35.

7   SG Nicholls, *Romanesque Signs: Early Medieval Narrative and Iconography* (Yale 1983) 16.

8   JC Dickinson, *The Origins of the Austin Canons and their Introduction into England* (London 1950), esp. 255-72; L Verhiejen, *La Règle de Sint Augustin*, 2 vols (Paris 1976); A Zumkeller, *Augustine's Ideal of the Religious Life* (Fordham 1986); G Lawless (ed.), *Augustine of Hippo and his Monastic Rule* (Oxford 1987).

9   Dickinson, *Origins of the Austin Canons*, 78, 86-7.

10 J Longère (ed.), *L'abbaye parisienne de Saint-Victor au moyen âge* (Turnhout 1991).

11 C Platt, *The Abbeys and Priories of Medieval England* (London 1984) 28-9.

12 See WM Kibler and GA Zinn (eds), *Medieval France, An Encyclopedia* (London & New York 1995) 848-49.

13 The most comprehensive account of the Irish Church in the age of reform is A Gwynn, *The Irish Church in the 11th and 12th centuries* (Dublin 1992).

14 Bernard, in his *Vita* of Malachy, states that Malachy founded a house for regular canons, probably at Bangor, 'according to his custom' (HJ Lawlor, *Saint Bernard of Clairvaux's Life of St Malachy of Armagh* (London 1920) 69.

15 For a discussion and references, see T O'Keeffe, 'Lismore and Cashel: reflections on the beginnings of Romanesque architecture in Munster, *RSAI Jn.*, 124 (1994) 135-8.

16 Discussed in Gwynn, *The Irish Church*.

17 For the introduction of these orders, see Gwynn and Hadcock, *Religious Houses: Ireland, passim.*

18 For the introduction of the Arroasians, see PJ Dunning, 'The Arroasian order in medieval Ireland', *IHS* 4 (1945) 297-315; also M-T Flanagan, 'St Mary's Abbey, Louth, and the introduction of the Arrouaisian observance into Ireland', *Clogher Record*, 10, 2 (1980) 223-34.

19 J Burton, *Monastic and Religious Orders in Britain, 1000-1300* (Cambridge 1994) 28; the fourth was Sherborne, abandoned in favour of Old Sarum. Of the late 11th and early 12th-century Irish bishops-elect, Patrick and Donnagus of Dublin were, respectively, monks at Worcester and Canterbury, and Malchus of Waterford was a monk at Winchester: J Watt, *The Church in Medieval Ireland* (Dublin 1972) 3.

20 Burton, *Monastic and Religious Orders*, 28.

21 Flanagan, 226 for Louth; see Gwynn and Hadcock, *Religious Houses: Ireland*, 149-51, and KW Nicholls, 'Medieval Irish Cathedral chapters', *Archivium Hibernicum*, 31 (1973) 102-11 for different perspectives on this.

22 Dickinson, *Origins of the Austin Canons*, 98-103.

23 Gwynn and Hadcock, *Religious Houses: Ireland*, 153-6.

24 J Watt, *The Church in Medieval Ireland* (London 1970) 4-8.

25 Dickinson, *Origins of the Austin Canons*, 111-12; for the Irish estates, see E St John Brooks (ed.), *The Irish Cartularies of Llanthony Prima and Secunda*, Irish Manuscripts Commission (Dublin 1953).

26 Burton, *Monastic and Religious Orders*, 23; Platt, *Abbeys and Priories of England*, ch 1.

27 R Gem, 'The English parish church in the 11th and 12th centuries: a great rebuilding?' in J Blair (ed.), *Minsters and Parish Churches: The Local Church in Transition 950-1200* (Oxford 1988) 21-30.

28 Unlike in the Benedictine and Cluniac congregations, 'priory' does not denote a dependent or subordinate status, but is usually an indication of the size of a community and its endowments, and therefore of its status.

29 J Ware, *De Hibernica, et Antiquitatibus ejus* (Dublin 1624) [W Harris (ed), 1739].

30 Based on Gwynn and Hadcock, *Religious Houses: Ireland*.

31 It was rare for communities themselves to take the initiative here: in the case of St Botulphs, Colchester – the first Augustinian house in England – the priests resident in what had been an Anglo-Saxon minster church sought advice on the embracing of regular life from one of their number who had studied at Bec, and he told them that 'there is in foreign parts a certain way of life wise and fine enough, but entirely unknown in these parts – the life and rule, that is to say, confirmed by the authority of the most holy Augustine, the glorious doctor, which furthermore is termed by Catholics the canonical rule.' See Dickinson, *Origins of the Austin Canons*, 99.

32 R Southern, *Western Society and the Church in the middle ages* (Harmondsworth 1970) 240-50.

33 DM Robinson, *The Geography of Augustinian Settlement*, 2 vols (Oxford 1980) 18-19.

34 Platt, *Abbeys and Priories of England*, 37-8.

35 Empey, 'Kells in Ossory', 137.

36 For a comprehensive discussion of the Anglo-Norman 'invasion' of Ireland, its background and its immediate aftermath, see FX Martin, 'Diarmait MacMurchada and the coming of the Anglo-Normans' and 'Allies and an overlord, 1169-72', in A Cosgrove (ed.), *A New History of Ireland II: Medieval Ireland 1169-1534* (London 1987) 43-125. One contemporary Irish annalist recorded the Norman arrival in rather terse language: 'A large body of knights came overseas to MacMurchada' (*Annals of Tigernach*, W Stokes (ed.), *Revue Celtique* (1895-97) *sub anno* 1169).

37 Giraldus Cambrensis, *Expugnatio Hibernica: the Conquest of Ireland*, AB Scott and FX Martin (eds) (Dublin 1978) 87.

38 A long-neglected area, the early history of Anglo-Norman settlement in Cork is now well served by H Jeffries, 'The founding of Anglo-Norman Cork, 1177-1185', *Cork Hist. Soc. Jn.*, 91 (1986) 26-48; by P McCotter, 'The sub-infeudation and descent of the Fitzstephen/Carew moity of Desmond', *Cork Hist. Soc. Jn.*, 101 (1996) 64-80; 102 (1997) 89-133; and by a new, comprehensively annotated edition of *The Pipe Roll of Cloyne* (*Rotulus Pipæ Clonensis*), KW Nicholls and P McCotter (eds) (Cloyne 1996).

39 It is possible, but less likely, as McCotter argues ('Subinfeudation and descent', 89), that the cantred was divided into these two parts by Robert fitz Stephen, and that it was he who made the grant of the western moity to the brothers fitz Hugh.

40 *Expugnatio*, 156.

41 E St John Brooks, 'Unpublished charters relating to Ireland', *RIA Proc.*, 62 (1936) 36.

42 Based on KW Nicholls, 'The development of lordship in Co Cork, 1300-1600' in P O'Flanagan and C Buttimer (eds), *Cork History and Society* (Dublin 1993) fig. 6.1.

43 O'Connell Redmond, 'Alexander Fitz Hugh', 169.

44 Synolda may have married David de Roche, a witness to a charter regarding lands near Glanworth in the 1230s; McCotter, 'Subinfeudation and descent', 104, n127.

45 Jeffries, 'Anglo-Norman Cork', 30-1, argues this against the testimony of Giraldus, who says the Normans were honourably received.

46 Mottes are strikingly absent from western and southern parts of the Norman colony, including Cork (RE Glasscock, 'Mottes in Ireland', *Château Gaillard*, 7 (1975) 95-110). The suggestion that another type of earth and timber castles – the ringwork castle – might have been used in these areas (D Twohig, 'Norman ringwork castles', *Bulletin of the Group for the Study of Irish Historic Settlement*, 5 (1978) 7-9; TB Barry, 'Anglo-Norman ringwork castles: some evidence' in T Reeves-Smyth and F Hammond (eds), *Landscape Archaeology in Ireland* (Oxford 1983) 295-314) has merit, but there are *a priori* objections to the model, and archaeological evidence is not forthcoming; see T O'Keeffe, 'The archaeology of Anglo-Norman castles in Ireland. Part 1: Mottes and ringworks', *Archaeology Ireland*, 4, 3 (Autumn 1990) 15-17. Early stone castles in the Cork area include Ballyderown, a hall of *c.*1200 in which the windows had Romanesque mouldings; see T O'Keeffe, 'An early Anglo-Norman castle at Ballyderown, county Cork', *RSAI Jn.*, 114 (1984) 48-56.

47 E St John Brooks, 'Unpublished charters', *passim*.

48 Jeffries, 'Anglo-Norman Cork', 33.

49 A Gwynn, 'The early history of St Thomas' Abbey, Dublin', *RSAI Jn.*, 84 (1954) 1-35.

50 D Knowles and RN Hadcock, *Medieval Religious Houses: England and Wales*, 2nd ed. (London 1971) 65.

51 The land of the parish of Marmullane and of the townland of Balilannocan were granted to St Nicholas in Exeter by fitz Stephen and de Cogan; de Cogan granted a knight's fee to St Thomas's in his cantred of Cinél nAedha (Kinalea), and also land on the border between Kerrycurrihy and Cinél nAedha was granted to the Cistercians of St Mary's Dublin. De Cogan's brother Richard granted possession of a church in Cinél nAedha to St Nicholas's, while his daughter, Margaret, granted two knight's fees from Uí Badhamhna (Ibawn and Barryroe baronies) and the church of Clonmel on Great Island with its appurtenances to St Thomas's, and twenty carucates (ploughlands) and all associated tithes in the cantred of Ros Ailithre to St Mary's in Dublin. Robert fitz Stephen granted to St Nicholas's three townlands and ten carucates beside his castle, possibly on Great Island. Alexander fitz Maurice, enfeoffed of Oglaissan by fitz Stephen, granted the church of Killeigh to St Thomas's. See Jeffries, 'Anglo-Norman Cork'.

52 Jeffries, 'Anglo-Norman Cork', 37; O'Connell Redmond, 'Alexander Fitz Hugh', 170.

53 Gwynn and Hadcock, *Religious Houses: Ireland, passim*.

54 Jeffries, 'Anglo-Norman Cork', 32.

55 *ibid.*, 34.

56 For a discussion of the participation of canons regular in parochial duties, see Dickinson, *Origins of Austin Canons*,

214-23.

[57] See MJC Buckley, 'The abbey of Molana', *RSAI Jn.*, 33 (1903) 313-4; P Power, 'The abbey of Molana, Co Waterford', *RSAI Jn.*, 62 (1932) 142-52. An effigy, now lost, of a knight, possibly Raymond le Gros, was recorded by Daniel Grose; see R Stalley (ed.), *Daniel Grose (c.1766-1838): The Antiquities of Ireland* (Dublin 1991) 11.

[58] For one demonstration of the complexity of the process of foundation, see JC Dickinson, 'The origins of St Augustine's, Bristol', in P Cannon and J McGrath (eds), *Essays in Bristol and Gloucestershire History* (Bristol and Gloucestershire Archaeological Society, 1976) 109-26. The regularity with which the sites of earlier monastic foundations were chosen by Augustinians and Cistercians is analysed in G Carville, *The Occupation of Celtic Sites in Ireland by the Canons Regular of St Augustine and the Cistercians*, Cistercian Studies Series 56 (Kalamazoo 1982).

[59] Several editions of the 1290 Inspeximus have been published: W Dugdale, *Monastici Anglicani. Volumen Alterum de Canonicus Regularibus Augustinianis* (London 1661) 1045-6, contains a Latin recension, while English translations are published in *Calendar of Documents relating to Ireland..., 1171-[1307]* HS Sweetman and GF Handcock (eds), 5 vols (London 1875-86) 3 (1285-92) 232-3, no. 587, and *Calendar of Charter Rolls... 1226-[1516]* (London 1903-27) 2 (1257-1300) 341. The 1334 Inspeximus is held in the Bodleian Library, Oxford (Rawlinson B 499 fol. 125v).

[60] In this year Bishop Simon de Rochfort changed the diocesan centre for Meath from Clonard to Newtown Trim (Gwynn and Hadcock, *Religious Houses: Ireland*, 97).

[61] Master Philip de Prendergast – not given in this recension.

[62] The Dugdale recension is in the first person – Alexander himself speaks – while the other two (*Cal. Doc. Ire.* and *Cal. Charter Rolls*) are in third person.

[63] This name is not given in the Dugdale version of the charter.

[64] Platt, *Abbeys and Priories of England*, 32.

[65] For Mellifont, see Stalley, *Cistercian Monasteries*, 57. The Buttevant crypt is a sophisticated work of architecture, and it may well have had a liturgical function similar to, say, the crypt of Glasgow Cathedral, where shrines of St Kentigern were kept.

[66] For the bridge, see C Power in *Mallow Field Club Jn.*, 6 (1988) 48.

[67] Patent Rolls 34, 8th April 1311: Royal Irish Academy Windele MS 12 1 14, 96.

[68] S Reynolds, *Kingdoms and Communities in Western Europe 900-1300* (Oxford 1984) 103-4.

[69] In the context of Tristernagh Priory, an Augustinian house in the midlands, the vill of Kilbixy is recorded as having had a toft granted from it, thus suggesting a settlement also; B Eager, 'Tristernagh Priory: the establishment of a colonial monastic house in the lordship of Meath' in WJ Sheils and D Wood (eds), *The Churches, Ireland and the Irish*, Studies in Church History, 25 (Oxford 1989) 31.

[70] *Calendar of Justiciary Rolls... of Ireland..: Edward I [1295-1307]* J Mills (ed.), 2 vols (Dublin 1905-14) 1 (1295-1303) 265. For the background to this list – the problem of 'false money' in the colony – see HF Berry (ed.), *Statutes and Ordinances and Acts of the Parliament of Ireland: King John to Henry V* (Dublin 1907) 213-5, 221-3; see also AF O'Brien, 'Politics, economy and society: the development of Cork and the Irish south-coast region c.1170 to c.1583' in P O'Flanagan and CG Buttimer (eds), *Cork, History and Society* (Dublin 1993) 133.

[71] *Cal. Justic. Rolls*, 1308-14, 295.

[72] KW Nicholls, 'The early Keatings', *The Irish Genealogist* 5 (1976) 286-7.

[73] The 1290 Inspeximus gives this as *domus* (house); the 1334 Inspeximus as *dominium*, lordship or demesne.

[74] O'Connell Redmond, 'Alexander Fitz Hugh', 169.

[75] Similar provisions were made for Tristernagh, for example, *Registrum cartarum monasterii BV Mariae de Tristernagh*, MV Clarke (ed.) (Dublin 1941) part 2 no. 8 (charter of Bishop Simon de Rochford of Meath).

[76] *Reg. Tristernagh*, xii-xiii.

[77] The eldest son and heir of Maurice de Prendergast, he had been enfeoffed by Philip de Barry in Ocurblethan, a great fief encompassed by a rural deanery of the same name, and established a borough at Shandon. He died in 1226; see O'Connell Redmond, 'Alexander FitzHugh', 170; Jeffries, 'Anglo-Norman Cork', 40.

[78] The second son of William de Barry and brother of Gerald of Wales, he arrived from Manorbier in Wales in 1183 to take possession of his grant of Olethan, which Ralph fitz Robert (Margaret de Cogan's wife, and son of Robert fitz Stephen) had given him. Carrigtwohill was probably the *caput* of this holding; O'Connell Redmond, 'Alexander FitzHugh', 170; Jeffries, 'Anglo-Norman Cork', 40.

[79] The de Kantitune (de Caunteton) brothers were nephews of Raymond le Gros, whose sister married Nicholas de Caunteton; their son, Raymond de Kantitone, was killed in Idrone according to Giraldus; McCotter, 'Subinfeudation and descent', 89.

[80] McCotter, 'Subinfeudation and descent', 39.

[81] For a comprehensive discussion, see B Thompson, 'From 'Alms' to 'Spiritual Services': the function and status of monastic property in medieval England' in J Loades (ed.), *Monastic Studies II: The Continuity of Tradition* (Bangor 1991) 227-262; see also T Burrows, 'Monastic benefactors in medieval Yorkshire', *Journal of Religious History*, 12 (1982-3) 3-8.

[82] In 1070, Bishop Ermenfrid of Sitten wrote that 'Anyone who does not know the number of those he wounded or killed [at Hastings] must, at the discretion of his bishop, do penance for one day in each week for the remainder of his life; or, if he can, let him redeem his sin by a perpetual alms, either by building or endowing a church.' DC Douglas and GW Greenaway, *English Historical Documents 1042-1189* (London 1953) 606-7.

83 Southern, *Western Society and the Church*, 225-8.

84 See Thompson, 'Monastic property in medieval England', 240-6.

85 In 1280, for example, a fine of half a mark was received from the prior of Bridgetown for licence to obtain an amended writ (*Cal. Doc. Ire.*, ii (1252-84) 360, no. 1740).

86 Thompson, 'Monastic property in medieval England', 248-9.

87 The making of this *Inspeximus* or copy of the original charter had been in response to a request to the king in 1289 from the prior and convent of Bridgetown for confirmation of their foundation charters from Alexander fitz Hugh.(*Cal. Doc. Ire.*, iii (1285-92) 249, no. 558). At this time, the community also requested letters of protection from the king, for which the response was that it would be kept 'in its right' by the king's justices. The community further requested that lands, rents, and churches, which were alienated by their priors without assent of the convent (contrary to the letter and spirit of the foundation charter), may be restored with the king's assistance, but they were advised to seek the restoration of these properties by writ. Finally, the community also pleaded for the sparing of their poor tenants of service on juries and assizes except those involving cases of rape, arson, forestal and treasure trove, but this request was refused as it was contrary to 'common justice'.

88 *Cal. Doc. Ire.*, ii (1252-84) 76, no. 470. That the convent should seek an Inspeximus of its charter because previous priors had alienated property is less surprising in view of the record of priors, or at least of one prior, in the 1280s for incurring fines for trespass. (*Cal. Doc. Ire.*, iii (1285-92) 55, no. 149 (1985); *ibid.*, 98, no. 215 (1286); *ibid.*, 124, no. 271 (1286); *ibid.*, 153, no. 330 (1287); *ibid.*, 167, no. 371 (1288) but once, in 1285, the fine is 106s 8d (*Cal. Doc. Ire.*, iii (1285-92) 190, no. 434 (1285). It may be pertinent to note that in 1302 a Brother Robert le Erseekene of the priory is recorded as having actually paid a fine of 20s for trespass (*Cal. Doc. Ire.*, v (1302-7) 37, no. 72).

89 That the foundation was for the soul of John is reiterated several times (*Cal. Doc. Ire.*, ii (1252-84) 76, no. 470, AD 1255; *Cal. Doc. Ire.*, iii (1285-92) 249, no. 558, AD 1289).

90 Thompson, 'Monastic property in medieval England', 255-7.

91 *Cal. Doc. Ire.*, v (1302-7) 42-3, no. 83; 50, no. 120; *Calendar of the Patent Rolls... 1232-[1509]*, 53 vols (London 1891-1971) 5 (1301-1307) 57.

92 Tristernagh had as benefactors the important families of Meath; see Eager, 'Tristernagh', 29.

93 Trinity College Dublin MS F 1. 15, 92; also K Nicholls, 'Early Keatings'.

94 In 1255, for example, the priory held two carucates of land in Fennor in Kildare (*Cal. Doc. Ire.*, ii (1252-84) 76, no. 470).

95 TCD MS F 1. 15, 92.

96 *Calendar of entries in the papal registers relating to Great Britain and Ireland*, 9 (1431-47) 74; *ibid.*, 13 (1471-84) 174; *ibid.*, 14 (1484-92) 238-9; *ibid.*, 14 (1484-92) 471, no. 875-6; *ibid.*, 15 (1492-1498) 102, no. 142; *ibid.*, 15 (1492-1498) 502,

97 MacCarthy, 'Norman Times', 135.

98 *Cal. Doc. Ire.*, i (1171-1251) 216, no. 1432-3; also *Cal. Patent Rolls*, 1226, 55.

99 *Cal. Doc. Ire.*, iii (1285-92) 55, no. 149 (1985); *ibid.*, 98, no. 215 (1286); *ibid.*, 124, no. 271 (1286); *ibid.*, 153, no. 330 (1287); *ibid.*, 167, no. 371 (1288).

100 *ibid.*, iii (1285-92) 190, no. 434 (1285).

101 *ibid.*, v (1302-7) 37, no. 72.

102 Grove White, 'Bridgetown Parish', 308.

103 *Cal. Doc. Ire..*, v (1302-7) 42-3, no. 83.

104 *Cal. Just. Rolls*, ii (1305-7) 332.

105 *Cal. Papal Reg.*, 2 (1305-42) 228.

106 *ibid.*, 4 (1362-1404) 86.

107 Grove White, 'Bridgetown Parish', 308.

108 Grove White, 'Bridgetown Parish', 308.

109 Grove White, 314.

110 Five years later it is revealed that it is void by the death of John Walcoe (*Cal. Papal Reg.*, 14 (1484-92) 119).

111 *ibid.*, 13 (1471-84) 719.

112 *ibid.*, 13 (1471-84) 174, 188. He is granted a canonry of Cloyne and the prebend of Ballyhooly from which John Whit and William Cwssin, clerks or priests without canonical title, are to be removed having respectively detained them; see also *ibid.*, 13 (1471-84) 174.

113 *ibid.*, 14 (1484-92) 119.

114 *ibid.*, 14 (1484-92) 119.

115 *ibid.*, 14 (1484-92) 238-9.

116 *ibid.*, 14 (1484-92) 471, no. 875-6.

117 He is still involved – he 'resigns' the priorship in 1493. *ibid.*, 15 (1492-1498) 102, no. 142.

118 *ibid.*, 15 (1492-1498) 502, no. 740.

119 *ibid.*, 15 (1492-1498) 102, no. 142.

120 *ibid.*, 15 (1492-1498) 250, no. 347.

121 *ibid.*, 15 (1492-1498) 106, no. 146.

122 *ibid.*, 15 (1492-1498) 250, no. 347.

123 *ibid.*, 15 (1492-1498) 502, no. 740.

124 *Cal. Patent and Close Rolls I (Henry VIII, Edward VI, Mary and Elizabeth)* 117; given as 1545 by Grove White, 'Bridgetown Parish', 308, citing Fiant 462, and pension given as £6 13s 4d.

125 When, for example, a request is made in 1363 for Nicholas, son of a Cistercian monk of *de choro benedicto* (Midleton) to be promoted to abbot, it was noted that Ireland had few persons 'fit for such dignities' (*Cal. Papal Reg.*, 1 (1342-1419) 467-8).

126 Unlike among the Cistercians for whom there needed to be thirteen in order to establish a new monastic foundation, there was no prescribed number of canons in an Augustinian house.

127 1449-50: (*Cal. Papal Reg.*, 10 (1447-55) 454); 1450 (*ibid.*, 10 (1447-55) 456; 1456: (*ibid.*, 11 (1455-64) 304) 1457: (*ibid.*, 11 (1455-64) 325); 1458: (*ibid.*, 12 (1458-71) 23 and *ibid.*, 12 (1458-71) 25); 1467: (*ibid.*, 12 (1458-71) 565 and *ibid.*, 12 (1458-71) 569); 1470: (*ibid.*, 12 (1458-71) 358; *ibid.*, 12 (1458-

71) 368 and *ibid.*, 12 (1458-71) 778); 1470-1: (*ibid.*, 12 (1458-71) 796); 1473: (*ibid.*, 13 (1471-84) 350); 1475: (*ibid.*, 13 (1471-84) 407, *ibid.*, 13 (1471-84) 421 and *ibid.*, 13 (1471-84) 435); 1477: (*ibid.*, 13 (1471-84) 578); 1484: (*ibid.*, 13 (1471-84) 182); 1484-5: (*ibid.*, 14 (1484-92) 80); 1502: (*ibid.*, 17, part 1 (1495-1503) 616, no. 1000); 1504: (*ibid.*, 18 (1503-13) 307-8, no. 376). There are also three references to papal mandatories around 1400: 1397 (*ibid.*, 5 (1396-1404) 151); 1400 (*ibid.*, 5 (1396-1404) 451); 1401: (*ibid.*, 5 (1396-1404) 448).

[128] J Harper, *The Forms and Orders of Western Liturgy from the Tenth to the Eighteenth Century* (Oxford 1991) is a useful account of liturgical activity in the medieval and early modern Church.

[129] The use of the western end for liturgical purposes was not unknown in the early medieval church, but by the end of the 11th century, liturgical functions were concentrated in the eastern arm of the church and the crossing, and by the time these great monastic churches reached Ireland, this transformation had happened.

[130] Harper, *Western Liturgy*, 36-7, 74.

[131] W Horn and E Born, *The Plan of St Gall* (Berkeley 1979).

[132] At Canon Island, Co Clare, a claustral monastery was built within a circular enclosure of the type normally inhabited by early monasteries; TJ Westropp, 'Prehistoric remains (forts and dolmens) in the Burren and its south western border', *RSAI Jn.*, 45 (1915) 271.

[133] D Waterman, 'Somersetshire and other foreign building stone in medieval Ireland', *UJA* 33 (1970) 63-75.

[134] J Bony, *The English Decorated Style* (Oxford 1979); N Coldstream, *The Decorated Style* (London 1994).

[135] G Crotty, 'Armorial seals in the Ormond archives: an important source for the study of heraldry in Ireland', *Genealogica & Heraldica* (Helsinki 1984) 269.

[136] G Coppock, *Abbeys and Priories* (London 1990) 67-72

[137] Stalley, *Cistercian Monasteries of Ireland*, 172

[138] Twohig revealed stretches of walling on the north and west sides of the cloister [**26**]. A line of stones was exposed running north-south and continuing the line of the exterior of the arcuated wall, which today defines the west side of the cloister passage. According to notes on the plan, three to four courses of this wall survived. The return of this wall along the north side of the cloister was also revealed: here it ran westwards for 3.5m as a double-faced wall, 90cm thick, before petering out. In the north-west corner of the court, in or close to the position in which one would expect to find the return of the inner cloister wall, a block of walling, measuring 1.5m by 1.7m and running north-south, was exposed. Twohig evidently did not consider this part of the medieval cloister, marking it 'function unknown' and 'post-medieval' on his plan. The final stretch of walling exposed ran northwards for 12.5m from the north wall of the south range, immediately east of the entrance into the refectory undercroft. Most of the length of this is comprised of a single line of stones facing eastwards; the northern 1.5m of

the wall is double-faced. Running parallel and at right angles to the church and refectory, the walls are probably the remains of an inner ambulatory wall; indeed the walling which runs north-south along the west side of the cloister runs towards the refectory on the east side of the latter's large doorway, which is in the position in which one would expect to find the inner ambulatory wall. Twohig's plan indicates that this putative ambulatory wall ran up to and abutted the refectory wall, and this suggests that there was no ambulatory passage running along this side of the refectory. We cannot say if any of these walls were still standing when the present east range and associated passage were built later in the 13th century.

In the cloister court, outside both the entrance to the refectory undercroft and the laver, Twohig also found a rectangular structure which he labelled a 'double stone walled pit, 1.5m+ deep' on his plan. Aligned north-south along the line of the western cloister walk, it measured about 4m by 2.7m internally, with a partition wall dividing it into two parts, the northern part measuring 1.6m north-south and the southern part 1.7m. The walls were about 60cm thick. Twohig wrote on his plan that this structure is possibly post-medieval in date. Its function is unknown, but its location immediately outside the refectory entrance and the lavatorium, both 13th century, suggests it is quite late in the priory's history.

[139] For examples of 'dumb-bell' piers, see Stalley, *Cistercian Monasteries*, ch 8.

[140] See T Crofton Croker, *Researches in the South of Ireland* (London 1824) 133 for illustrations of other examples now lost.

[141] G Coppack, *Abbeys and Priories*, 69.

[142] In 1995 the upper stones courses were taken down as a means of stabilising the building.

[143] These stones have all been numbered and a descriptive catalogue lodged with Cork County Council.

[144] N Coldstream, *Masons and Sculptors* (London 1991); D Knoop and GP Jones, *The Medieval Mason* 3rd ed. (Manchester 1967).

[145] Coppack, *Abbeys and Priories*, 46.

[146] A useful summary is provided by Coldstream, *Masons and Sculptors*, 37-8; P Kidson, 'A metrological investigation', in *Courtauld Warburg Inst. Jn.*, 53 (1990) 71-97. For a demonstration of how such proportions dictate the plan design of medieval architecture, see P Kidson, 'The historical circumstances and the principles of the design' in T Cocke and P Kidson, *Salisbury Cathedral. Perspectives on the Architectural History* (London 1993) 35-91.

[147] Gwynn and Hadcock, *Religious Houses: Ireland*, 102-8.

[148] O'Keeffe, 'Lismore and Cashel'.

[149] T O'Keeffe, 'Cashel' in A Simms and JH Andrews (eds) *More Irish Country Towns* (Cork 1995) 169.

[150] Stalley, *Cistercian Monasteries*, 14-20.

[151] C Waddell, 'The reform of the liturgy from a renaissance perspective' in RL Benson and G Constable (eds), *Renaissance and Renewal in the Twelfth Century* (Oxford 1982) 106.

[152] Peter the Venerable mocked its fierce rejection of the trappings

of contemporary Christianity. He wrote 'O new race of Pharisees, who to distinguish yourselves from the other monks of almost the entire world, lay claim to a habit of unwonted colour to show that you are white while the rest are black'; Lawrence, *Medieval Monasticism*, 148.

[153] In 1157, the General Chapter, the body which was charged with the running of the Order from the mid-1120s, issued a prohibition on the building of church towers (Stalley, *Cistercian Monasteries*, 141). This was the first specific statute concerning architecture. There were no guidelines on architecture from the General Chapter during Bernard's lifetime, and this suggests that whatever opinions he had on the nature of churches, they were not radical when measured against the views of his fellow Cistercians.

[154] Yet it is curious that Robert's builders produced a church at Mellifont which, in elements of its ground plan at least, was quite unlike that at Clairvaux, and indeed Mellifont's daughter house, Baltinglass, was also different from both its Mellifont and Clairvaux, indicating that, right from the outset, even within this most consistent of monastic orders, the Irish location produced individuality.

[155] O von Simson, *The Gothic Cathedral* (2nd ed. Princeton 1972) *passim.*

[156] A number of these Augustinian foundations have been adequately published. Of those illustrated in figure 99, see TJ Westropp, 'The Augustinian houses of County Clare: Clare, Killone and Inchicronan', *RSAI Jn.*, 30 (1900) 118-35 for the three Clare monasteries; for Ballinskelligs see A O'Sullivan and J Sheehan (eds), *The Iveragh Peninsula, An Archaeological Survey of South Kerry* (Cork 1996) 347-51; for Ferns see R Cochrane, *Ferns, County Wexford*. Extract from the 78th Annual Report of the Commissioners of Public Works in Ireland (Dublin 1910); for Killagha see J Carmody, 'The abbey of Killagha, Parish of Kilcoleman, County Kerry', *RSAI Jn.* 36 (1906) 285-96; for Kells see D Tietzsch-Tyler, *The Augustinian Priory of Kells, Co Kilkenny: An Exploration* (Freshford 1993); for Monasternagalliaghduff see J Wardell, 'The history and antiquities of St Catherine's, Old Abbey, County Limerick', *RSAI Jn.*, 34 (1904) 41-64; for Inchcleraun see FJ Bigger, 'Inis Clothran (Inis Cleraun), Lough Ree: its history and antiquities', *RSAI Jn.*, 30 (1900) 69-90; for Athassel see R Cochrane, 'Notes on the Augustinian Priory of Athassel, County Tipperary', *RSAI Jn.*, 39 (1909) 279-80; for Ballybeg see M Shine, 'Ballybeg Priory', *Mallow Field Club Jn.*, 11 (1993) 84-112, and 12 (1994) 89-114; and for Clontuskert see T Fanning, 'Clontuskert Priory, Co Galway', *RIA Proc.*, 76 C (1976) 97-169.

[157] See TW Bizzaro, *Romanesque Architectural Criticism, A Prehistory* (Cambridge 1992).

[158] O'Keeffe, 'Lismore and Cashel'.

[159] *ibid.*

[160] For history, see GJ Hand, The rivalry of the cathedral chapters in medieval Dublin, *RSAI Jn.,* 92 (1962) 193-206; A Gwynn, 'The origins of the see of Dublin', *IER,* 57 (1941) 169-96.

[161] O'Keeffe, 'Ballyderown'.

[162] A full survey was published by GE Street and E Seymour, *The Cathedral of the Holy Trinity, commonly called Chrish Church Cathedral, Dublin: an Account of the Restoration of the Fabric* (London 1882).

[163] Illustrations from Street and Seymour, *Holy Trinity.*

[164] O'Keeffe, 'Lismore and Cashel'.

[165] T Drew, 'The ancient chapter-house of the priory of the Holy Trinity, Dublin', *RSAI Jn.*, 20 (1890-1) 36-43; T Drew, 'On evidence of the plan of the cloister garth and monastic buildings of the priory of the Holy Trinity, now known as Christ Church Cathedral, Dublin', *RIA Proc.*, 16 (1879-86) 169.

[166] A Gwynn, 'Some unpublished texts from the Black Book of Christ Church, Dublin', *Analecta Hibernica* 16 (1946) 308-10.

[167] RA Stalley, 'The medieval sculpture of Chrish Church Cathedral, Dublin', *Archaeologia*, 106 (1979) 107-22.

[168] T Drew, 'The ancient chapter-house of the priory of the Holy Trinity, Dublin', *RSAI Jn.,* 20 (1890-1) 36-43.

[169] GJ Hand, 'The rivalry of the cathedral chapters in medieval Dublin', *RSAI Jn.,* 92 (1962) 193-206.

[170] R Cochrane, 'Notes on the Augustinian Priory of Athassal, County Tipperary', *RSAI Jn.,* 39 (1909) 279-89.

[171] Tietzsch-Tyler, *Kells.*

[172] RR Brash, 'An account of some antiquities in the neighbourhood of Buttevant, in the county of Cork', *RSAI Jn.*, 2 (1852) 265-72.

[173] A very similar tower survives at St Mary's, Askeaton, Co Limerick.

[174] HG Leask, *Irish Churches and Monastic Buildings III: Medieval Gothic – The Last Phases* (Dundalk 1965) 133-53.

[175] *Extents of Irish Monastic Possessions*, NB White (ed.) (Dublin 1943) 69.

[176] Grove White, 308; *Cal. Patent and Close Rolls I (Henry VIII, Edward VI, Mary and Elizabeth)* 117.

[177] *Cal. State Papers* (1509-73) 264-5.

[178] Fiants, 1107.

[179] Fiants, 3020, 3028.

[180] Grove White, 'Bridgetown parish', 305-6.

[181] *Cal. Patent and Close Rolls of Chancery,* ii, J Morrin (ed.) (London 1862) 158.

[182] Grattan-Flood, 'Bridgetown', 69.

[183] Fiants, 5911; Grove White, 309, adds, 'To hold for 50 years from the end of existing interests. He shall not charge coyn or livery.'

[184] C Roche, *The Ford of the Apples: A History of Ballyhooly* (Fermoy 1988) 69.